DEMOCRACY IN RETROGRADE

How to Make Changes Big and
Small in Our Country and in Our Lives

★ ★ ★ ★ ★ ★ ★ ★ ★

SAMI SAGE & EMILY AMICK

Gallery Books

New York   London   Toronto   Sydney   New Delhi

G

Gallery Books
An Imprint of Simon & Schuster, LLC
1230 Avenue of the Americas
New York, NY 10020

First Gallery Books hardcover edition July 2024

GALLERY BOOKS and colophon are registered trademarks of Simon & Schuster, LLC

Simon & Schuster: Celebrating 100 Years of Publishing in 2024

For information about special discounts for bulk purchases, please contact Simon & Schuster Special Sales at 1-866-506-1949 or business@simonandschuster.com.

The Simon & Schuster Speakers Bureau can bring authors to your live event. For more information, or to book an event, contact the Simon & Schuster Speakers Bureau at 1-866-248-3049 or visit our website at www.simonspeakers.com.

Interior design by Jason Snyder

Manufactured in the United States of America

10 9 8 7 6 5

Library of Congress Control Number: 2024932349

ISBN 978-1-6680-5348-5
ISBN 978-1-6680-5350-8 (ebook)

This book is dedicated to all those who have fought, and all those who ever will fight, for a more inclusive American democracy. We certainly wouldn't be legally permitted to write this book if it were not for you.

★ ★ ★

CONTENTS

SECTION 7:
ADDITIONAL RESOURCES

★

SECTION 1: INTRODUCTION

Why We're Here

THERE'S AN INTERESTING THING that happens when you develop a following on social media . . . people start telling you their most intimate thoughts.

After years of talking about news and politics on social media, we've heard from thousands of people who have shared something along the lines of: *I am scared/frustrated/feeling hopeless about our political situation. I want to do something but I don't know what to do.*

The seeds of what you're reading now were planted with an Instagram DM sent three days after the January 6 insurrection. Just as the Founding Fathers intended, we complimented each others anticoup content and exchanged predictions about what would happen next. (First conversation tip of the book! *Open with a compliment.*) Over the next few months, we bonded over our mutual passions (interior design, charming hotels, our dogs) and our constant frustrations (corrupt politicians, structural inequality, the general *Veep*-esque nature of everything).

Since then, we've spent a lot of late nights dissecting why and how America has gotten to this point. The result is the book you're holding in your hands, our attempt to share those conversations with you. *Democracy in Retrograde* is full of answers we wish we could include in our response to *every* DM, and our suggestions for pulling yourself out of the helplessness rut. It's a how-to guide for getting involved in a way that feels authentic and sustainable to *you*, ideally for longer than the average *Bachelor* Nation relationship. It's a guidebook to help you better understand why you feel the way you do, how you can gain a sense of control and ownership over your civic life, and how to make a plan to help you achieve *your* civic goals.

We believe that civic engagement is a form of self-care. Making your voice heard by your elected representatives and becoming engaged in your community are fundamental assertions of self-worth and self-esteem. In a democratic society, this is how you say, *I have a voice and the right to use it, and my contributions and beliefs matter.*

Our hope is that this book will inspire a lifelong internal paradigm shift, because civic engagement—whatever that looks like for you—is a reclamation of your place in a community, a statement of your values, and an act of self-respect.

Politics is probably the last place you'd expect to find a dose of self-help, but this isn't just a self-help book for you personally, it's chicken soup for America's soul. More people who care about their neighbors, who want to see positive changes, who get involved and push to improve the country, are what we need.

It may feel like everyone has extreme political opinions these days, but at least a third of American citizens are so disengaged in the democratic system that they didn't even vote in the 2020 presidential election. (Only 37 percent voted in all 3 of the major elections in 2018, 2020, and 2022).[1] Moreover, Americans are woefully disengaged in the politics of our own towns, cities, schools, and courts. And our policies and systems continue to be shaped by those who are most engaged, the loudest, and the already-powerful.

For democracy to function, we need more people who care about their communities to step up and help shepherd our country into the future. Preferably one that doesn't resemble *The Handmaid's Tale* or *The Day After Tomorrow*. We hope this book will help you get there.

Sorry—we should take a moment to introduce ourselves:

Sami: Many people might recognize me as one of the three cofounders of Betches Media, which I started alongside two of my childhood friends when we were seniors at Cornell University in 2011. What began as an anonymous satirical blog that we started with no commercial intent, has grown into a full multiplatform media business that we bootstrapped for 12 years without investors until our company was acquired by LBG Media in 2023. Though I've worn many different hats as a start-up founder, my one constant has been an intense focus on social media trends and messaging (no, I won't tell you my screen time, it's embarrassing). In the period before the 2016 election, we started Betches's news and politics vertical, with the mission of translating current events through a pop culture lens. Much like Connor Roy, I was interested in politics at a very young age, and I had long suspected that many of our elected officials behaved just like *Real Housewives* in suits. Betches News has since built a massive and highly engaged audience on the thesis that news content should be consumer-friendly. To that end, I record a daily news podcast called *Morning Announcements*, which delivers the key headlines in five minutes with some light commentary.

While my career has afforded me the privilege of contributing to this book, I can trace the seeds of some of its ideas to a conversation I overheard when I was nine years old. My brother Zachary, who was three years younger than me, was diagnosed with autism in the early 1990s, which is relevant because there was substantially less support and clarity around treatments for mental health and the disabled community than there is now. I was home sick from school one day, and I heard my mom begging an insurance company to cover one of Zach's very costly treatments, which my parents couldn't afford out-of-pocket. It wasn't the last time I heard my mother lobby for basic needs on my brother's behalf. School administrators, local government agencies, Medicaid. It has never escaped me that our individual fate is more in the hands of our collective society than many of us would like to admit, and I feel compelled to help improve our shared experience.

Emily: I'm a lawyer, journalist, and evangelist for the power of civic engagement. I'm known as @EmilyinYourPhone on social media, where I share the inside scoop about what's happening on Capitol Hill and the tools to advocate for political change. During my career I've worked at a nonprofit, an impact litigation firm, and the United States Senate as Judiciary Committee Counsel to (*as of this* *writing*) Senate Majority Leader Chuck Schumer. I've worked on some of the biggest legislation that's passed through Congress on both sides (as a staffer and an advocate) and have spent years honing my understanding of how to get sh-t done. Before I went to law school, I was a journalist. After a quick stint writing without sharing my opinions (it didn't last), I've since spent most of my life trying to think about how to take what I know and translate it in a way that empowers my friends to step into their political power. (PS. I love a parenthetical. Please see them as they are intended, an aside from me to you.)

Back to the book:

We've both built communities that care about politics, and everything we've been hearing from you has inspired this book. Talking about the news on social media isn't just about telling people what's happening, it's about making seemingly nonsensical things make sense. It's trying to explain why it's so hard to pass popular legislation (the filibuster) or parsing the labyrinth of voter registration deadlines and rules across fifty states every November. It's giving people a sense of agency in the complicated world of congressional gridlock and learning about the unique and specific ways that policies affect people's lives. It's about getting a DM where someone tells us how they themselves are involved in a story or in the political process.

None of that was part of the "How a Bill Becomes a Law" song from *Schoolhouse Rock!* But it's what "civics" was always supposed to be about.

If You're Thinking, *Civics? Really?*

MERRIAM-WEBSTER DICTIONARY defines "civics" as "a social science dealing with the rights and duties of citizens." "Civics" doesn't just need a rebrand, it needs whatever Julie Andrews did to make Anne Hathaway a suitable Prin*cess* of Genovia. That is: reveal the beauty that was already there and recast her in the light she should've been in all along.

The concept of civics can seem like a snooze when the conversation is divorced from its tangible effects on people's lives and from the community networks that bind people together. It's easy to forget that positively impacting *actual people* is supposed to be the point. Americans' ability to access the basic resources of a functioning society—clean air and water, safe buildings and infrastructure, security, housing, jobs, healthcare, roads, schools, and other assets that improve our quality of life and collective economic circumstances (for the capitalists in the back)—has often been obscured by other forces.

There's a small handful of very wealthy and powerful people who actively strategize and spend a lot of money (numbers with multiple commas) to make sure that you ignore politics and neglect your privileges that come with being an American citizen. You know that frustrated, helpless vibe we've all been feeling? It serves their purposes to have us checked out of politics, so the first step toward transforming pent-up anxiety into big, powerful change is reframing your relationship to civics and politics.

We think it's important to note up front that some people choose to disconnect from politics due to the historical harm inflicted by political institutions on their communities. We recognize that disengagement is both a valid form of protest and a necessary act of self-care. Our goal is to reach those who have disengaged not out of protest, but apathy.

We also recognize that everyone goes through seasons of their lives in which they have more or less that they can contribute. We're not here telling you to do 18,000 things tomorrow if you're already drowning. There are so many ways to be engaged in civic life: advocating for policy changes, joining a sports league, organizing a meal train for a sick neighbor, serving on a school board, or even trying to dismantle the entire system itself.

The thing we aim to tackle in this book is apathy. Apathy that results from giving up, tapping out, frustration, and hopelessness. We cannot treat civic engagement as if it's a TV series that we can drop after a few seasons when it becomes uninteresting (if you are still watching *Grey's Anatomy* we need you to turn that commitment to your local zoning board). Nothing changes when people think, *Everything is terrible and Mercury is always in retrograde, so why bother?*

Civic apathy is not merely an indicator of disinterest in politics; it's a symptom of a deeper disconnect with our shared American life. As community bonds weaken, so does our engagement with democracy. In today's fragmented, increasingly digital existence, our access to shared community wisdom and shared truths is frayed, replaced with information from isolated silos rooted in dubious and unverified claims. The transition from face-to-face gatherings to online interactions has changed the way we connect and engage, the way we perceive people from other groups, and the things people will reply to an online handle that they would never dare say in real life.

There have been many books written on political organizing tactics: how to build coalitions, how to create nonprofits, how to organize a grassroots movement, how to run for office. Those books exist for people who want to dig deeper into the mechanics of political action, but this book is for you.

Democracy in Retrograde is for everyone who wants to do their part to make our communities and country better but is also busy with their full-time job, caregiving for one or more generations of their family, running a business, managing their kids' schedules, minding their household finances, and more.

"You cannot take your freedoms for granted. Just like generations who have come before you, you have to do your part to preserve and protect those freedoms. . . . You need to be preparing yourself to add your voice to our national conversation. You need to prepare yourself to be informed and engaged as a citizen, to serve and to lead, to stand up for our proud American values and to honor them in your daily lives."

—MICHELLE OBAMA

In these pages, we will:

▸ Explain how the actions that strengthen our democracy are the same ones that will heal the loneliness and hopelessness many of us feel. The brokenness of our civic lives—the loss of connections and trust, an information ecosystem that heightens polarization, the concentration of power—results in frustration, hopelessness, and disillusion, which makes us tap out from civics entirely (Section 2).

▸ Dive into the hopelessness spiral that pulls us into despair and disengagement, and show how taking actions that are rooted in your personal values is the antidote to get yourself out of it (Section 3).

▸ Equip you to match your personality, skills, resources, interests, and values to meaningful actions within your community, whether you have only a few minutes to spare or are ready to make a lifetime commitment (Section 4).

▸ Provide functional exercises to get on track to building a civic life that's sustainable and authentic to you (Section 6).

▸ Give you our own version of *Schoolhouse Rock!* . . . a quick rundown on how the government really works, to inform your decisions on how to make the biggest impact with your time. Once you have an understanding of how the system works, it is easier to make a plan to change it (Additional Resources).

There are a bunch of exercises in the book intended to help you create a civic action plan that is authentic and sustainable to you:

▸ Initial reflection exercise: We can't tell you exactly what actions you should take; we want to help you find a path that is meaningful and sustainable for *you*. The first step is taking stock of where you're at, what issues bother or excite you, and what you will feel passionately about working towards in the long term (Section 1).

▸ Find your hope outlook (and reflection exercise): The thing we hear most often is that you feel hopeless. And we think that makes sense! We ask you to explore how your hope outlook shapes your engagement with politics (Section 2).

▸ Develop your personal mission statement: This exercise builds on the previous two to help you drill down on your values and your vision for your own civic engagement (Section 3).

▸ Discover your civic personality: Did you love taking a magazine quiz in your teens? Then you'll love this one. Each civic personality comes with action items and ideas for how you can engage with your community (Section 4).

▸ Audit your news consumption: Section 5 is full of practical tools to help you get started. We think starting with a news audit is step number one in coming up with an action plan (Section 5).

▸ Create your civic calendar: One of the things we hear from people is an intense pressure to know and do it all. We walk you through setting up a civic calendar that works for your life (Section 5).

▶ Build a civic network: When we think about fighting loneliness and setting you up for a sustainable civic future, friendships are the answer. We delve into building a civic network intentionally (Section 5).

▶ Assemble your civic action plan: As you do the exercises throughout this book, we'll be asking you to flip to the back and write in a few key pieces of information that result in final exercise which is your civic action plan. If you are just starting off and worried you don't know enough about politics to get there, please know the only prerequisite you need is caring about people's lives (your own, your family's, your community's, and beyond) (Section 5).

> A note: You do NOT have to read this book in order! Skip around to the sections you want to read. This is a choose your own adventure guide! Much like for many elected officials, there are no rules!

There's no such thing as too late to start, and there's no need to be ashamed if you've voted with the consistency of Kathleen Kelly in *You've Got Mail*. Those elections are over, those chads have been hung. Through sustained, collective efforts we can reverse the retrograde course of democracy and construct a society that upholds the principles of fairness, inclusivity, shared security, and prosperity. By reclaiming the power of the majority—your power— we can forge a future where the voice of the people truly reigns supreme. So, consider this your invitation to explore your passions and talents, to identify the issues that resonate deeply with you, and to find ways to contribute. *Cue Shania Twain.*

Initial Reflection Exercise

TO GET STARTED, we ask that you take stock of where you are in your civic journey today, reflect on your current engagement, and catalogue your interests.

We think this will help you figure out what type of civic plan would be both attainable and fulfilling to you. The goal isn't to dictate what actions to take, it's to help you clarify what is important to you. As you move through this book, you'll be asked more-precise questions about how you want to engage. Later, you'll be able to look back on your answers to the following set of questions so you can anchor your plan into something that addresses the concerns that are personal to you.

▶ What makes you stressed or anxious about politics? What keeps you up at night?

▶ What do you want to see change in this country (big picture)? If you had a magic wand, pick the first three things you would change.

▶ What do you want to see change in your local community? If you had a magic wand, pick the first three things you would change.

▶ Is there anything that you feel is missing from your life? A support system? Friends you can rely on? A sense of community? A way to relax? A way to give back? To simply meet your neighbors? A new hobby? A sense of belonging?

▶ How do you currently engage in civic life? In your town/community/country? (It's okay if the answer is *not at all.* That's why we're here!)

▶ If you have kids or hope to someday, what are some lessons you want to teach them about civic engagement? (Again, it's okay if you don't know. That's what we're going to figure out!)

▶ What kind of space and time do you have in your life currently? For example, do you want to add things to your life (new activities, relationships); change aspects of your present routine, interactions, or social circle; or learn how to engage while you're already burning the candle at both ends?

When you finish this exercise, go to page 179,
"Bringing It All Together," and write down a few notes.

SECTION 2:
DEMOCRACY IN RETROGRADE

Why Helping Democracy Will Also Give You a More Meaningful Life

FOR MANY PEOPLE, *politics* might be one of the dirtiest words in the English language, second only to *moist*. We know you probably have feelings about specific issues, but we'd argue that these (negative) feelings about our political system are also related to something bigger and harder to name.

It's the vibes. The vibes are off. Something is missing from American life.

In his renowned book *Bowling Alone* (2000), Harvard public policy professor Robert D. Putnam argued that there has been a precipitous decline of "social capital" in America. Social capital, as Putnam explains, is the fabric that binds our communities together. It's not something you can touch or see, but it's undeniably present in the connections between people. Think of social capital as the trust, goodwill, and cooperation that we foster within our relationships. When you lend something to a neighbor, attend a local town gathering, or simply greet someone with a smile, you're engaging in acts that build social capital.

SAMI SAGE & EMILY AMICK

As Putnam discusses in *Bowling Alone*, there has been a notable decline in face-to-face social interactions, leading to an erosion of social capital. Most famously, as reflected in his book's title, Putnam pointed to the decline in bowling leagues as a metaphor for social disengagement. While more people were bowling than ever before, league bowling dropped by 40 percent from 1970 to 1993. His research depicts a society that has lost many foundational opportunities for communal bonding, ushering in an era marked by isolation and detachment. He connected the dissolution of civic organizations like Lions Clubs and social groups like bowling leagues with the drop in social trust among Americans and warned of the negative impact it has on our individual and collective lives. He wrote, "The single most common finding from a half century's research on the correlates of life satisfaction, not only in the United States but around the world, is that happiness is best predicted by the breadth and depth of one's social connections."[1]

But it's not just the cratering of bowling leagues. Putnam highlighted that between 1965 and 2000, there was a 58 percent drop in attendance at club meetings, a 35 percent reduction in having friends over, and a 43 percent decrease in family dinners. This decline in socializing (within bowling leagues and more) represented a broader societal shift away from communal activities and toward individualism, socioeconomic stratification, and isolation.

According to Putnam, the loss of social capital is explained by the loss of what he and many scholars refer to as the "public square." A public square is more than just a physical location; it's a social construct, a gathering place where community members come together to meet, debate, gossip, and simply connect. It's the local church where neighbors meet every Sunday, the village center with community spaces (like town hall, the library, the post office, a public park), or the farmers' market where local economies are supported and personal connections are made. It's a space that fosters dialogue, nurtures relationships, and shapes community norms and values. Picture it like the mini-village that Kim Kardashian built for her kids, except it's the center of social and economic life for thousands of residents, not four billionaires under twelve.

Historically, these public squares were the lifeblood of civic engagement. People went to these places not just to run errands but to fill their lives with intangible connections. Like that sign in the library says, "People may go to the library looking mainly for information, but they find each other there."[2]

Lots of ink has been spilled analyzing the drop in community engagement. Scholars have posited that it's the result of many factors, including the rise of dual-income households, rising income inequality, less time for hobbies, and suburbanization. The lived experience of many of us today is that we have siloed individual relationships with like-minded people but increasingly limited in-person interactions with our own communities. And despite the promise of social media as a tool of connection and information, it comes along with its own slew of downsides, echo chambers, and an endless scroll of reasons to stay home rather than socialize in real life.

Since that first screech of a dial-up connection, the internet has fundamentally transformed how we interact with people whom we both live next door to and across the country from. Communication is certainly more efficient, but the social platforms on which we spend the most time are shaped by algorithms that reward hyper-niche subjects and/or strong emotional reactions. Rather than being exposed to new or different ideas online, we are technologically sorted into echo chambers where our own views are reinforced and heightened. Technology enables us to create the illusion of community and camaraderie without the challenges of sitting with other human beings and their messy (but beautiful) nuances. We lose the instinct to perceive those with whom we might disagree as merely holding a different (but valid) perspective, or as fellow flawed humans who inevitably hold some wrong opinions, as opposed to irredeemably evil monsters who are ruining America.

While the present antisocial era is surely an introvert's dream, it has coincided with a rise in national loneliness and isolation that makes individuals vulnerable to radicalization and increases their likelihood of joining extremist groups.[3] This problem has only gotten more severe as social media algorithms continue to incentivize fear and polarization for profit, while bad actors simultaneously become savvier and more organized in their approaches to manipulating these algorithms.

But back to in-person life for a second. "Third spaces" (places like churches and clubs) have historically offered a chance for individuals to share proximity without actively choosing it, making them incubators of social capital, empathy, and intergroup bonding. On the other hand, the loss of these free third spaces has only reinforced socioeconomic barriers, because when people must spend money to leave their house, they are likely going to interact primarily with people who spend money in similar ways, leading to further class stratification. Our lack of opportunities to socialize in unstructured, free-of-charge venues has limited our exposure to new people, and the ensuing acceptance of those who are dissimilar to us has declined in tandem. Exposure is humanizing, but we're increasingly short on these much needed experiences.

As terminally online people, we feel as if we are involved in an ongoing anthropological study. It's clear to us as users that while social media scratches the itch of social connection in our brains, it doesn't replace the benefits of genuine, in-person friends and con-nections.* Authentic connections keep us grounded in terms of how we perceive our own lives, the innate value of all human beings, and the facts about the world we live in.

Moreover, social media algorithms are at their most threatening when influencing individuals who feel lonely or rejected by society, creating echo chambers that amplify feelings of victimhood and blame, while simultaneously providing a simulacrum of a commu-nity full of people who confirm their (false and/or cult-friendly) perspectives. This is especially dangerous when someone has zero authentic real-world relationships to keep them tethered to reality in their offline hours.

The digital era has created a fascinating paradox: we experience more connectivity than our brains can handle yet feel lonelier than

---

* Though it's worth noting that this book wouldn't exist if we hadn't had a chance to meet thanks to social media. Ultimately, social media offers a ton of potential for real-life connection, and we hope this book helps you cultivate intentionality around pursuing it.

ever (see more on loneliness in the chapter on the civic personality Connectors). British anthropologist Robin Dunbar has posited that our brains can handle only 150 relationships, a number far exceeded by a nightly scroll on Instagram. The result is that people have many online connections, but the real ties—the ones that improve our quality of life—are fewer than ever. The loneliness epidemic is a public health crisis, and its correlation with our fracturing communities gets at the very heart of what it means to have a happy life—being cared for and caring for other people.

Increased civic engagement, though it sounds dry as toast, is not only a path to improving the health of our democracy and our own life satisfaction, but also a way to rebuild the uplifting parts of community life. This means intentionally making and maintaining connections with people near us who are invested in a shared future, even when we disagree on the specifics of how to get there.

While we might no longer be forced to farm with our neighbor to feed ourselves through the winter, we still share resources. *How should we run our schools? Our police? When should we repave our sidewalks?* At even larger scales, the act of policymaking is just village building. It's deciding the contours, pulleys, and levers of society. For example, America uses a system of taxes and fees to incentivize things we want (bigger families) and disincentivize things we want to halt (smoking, overweight luggage).

America is not alone in this melting of the civic fabric. Emily was recently in Scotland for Hogmanay (their New Year's Eve celebration), which is, truly, a BFD. For years there have been massive celebrations in Edinburgh and Glasgow, as well as in villages across the country. Speaking to Scottish people, though, Emily heard time and time again that their village had stopped the Hogmanay celebration. "We used to close down the square and everyone would go in and out of the bars," lamented a woman Emily met at a pub outside Fort William. "Now they stay home." The debauchery, the dancing, the shared experiences in the long, dark Scottish winters are facing the same fate as our proverbial bowling leagues.

And it makes sense—who can afford to get a babysitter for every night out and about? We are less likely to live near family members or trusted neighbors who can watch the kids for the night. Modernity has pushed us into isolation, but at least our TV and Wi-Fi are there, salves in our warm homes, offering the illusion of community connection. What Emily heard from folks in Scotland resonated with everything she has heard from friends in the U.S. for years. A yearning to live out that nostalgic fantasy of Stars Hollow–style neighborliness, but without the structural inequalities and regressive ideologies that others might hope to revisit when they romanticize those communities of yore (e.g.: tradwives).

Speaking of yore, some of our elected officials (we won't name names) would love to move back in time. They would love nothing more than for all of us to take a collective personal day, because we're just "not that political." Their ideal scenario is that we completely disengage from our communities, ceding the public square to whatever policies they want. It's no coincidence that the eras most frequently fetishized by extremist politicians are the ones associated with disenfranchisement and lack of civil rights. Such a future is far from impossible, and preventing it will require broad and deep collaboration, including and especially by people who have never been civically engaged before.

Even when you're motivated to make a change, it can be uncomfortable to get started. Getting involved in a new advocacy or political group, even just going to something like the school board meeting, often has first-day-at-a-new-school vibes: everyone else knows each other, where the bathroom is, and the lingo . . . and you don't. We've all started new jobs or been to a new school, or joined a new sporting team. The first time you go, it can be a bit disorienting, but you adjust. The goal is to find something that builds off what you already care about, the people that you want to help, and the communities you are enmeshed in. We believe that the time and effort (and a little discomfort) will ultimately add to your life in invaluable ways.

On Democracy:
A Work in Progress

DEMOCRACY IS A LIVING, breathing beast whose strength hinges on the full unhindered participation of all citizens.

Has America ever been a fully functioning democracy, or democratic republic? Absolutely not.

There was no democracy when Black people were enslaved. There was no democracy when women were legally classified as the property of their husbands. And a fully formed democracy did not suddenly unfold when those groups gained the right to vote. Though America has made strides toward a "more perfect union," it has never been fully achieved. Now, with the gutting of the Voting Rights Act and the overturning of *Roe v. Wade*, our democracy is in retrograde—turning back much of the progress made by previous generations.

Minority Rule: The Anti-Democracy

* * *

A major harbinger of this retrograde slide is the degree to which minority rule has infiltrated how we are governed at all levels. Minority rule has silenced the desires of the majority of Americans across several issues. It prevents the adoption of popular, commonsense policy changes. Minority rule has also heightened political polarization and allowed the wealthiest corporations to exploit workers for exploding profits and astronomical executive compensation.

All these conditions have blossomed into a garden of corruption, regulatory capture, and record levels of wealth inequality, and for the first time we've seen the shortening of the average American life span.[1] (Apropos of nothing, we're a lot of fun at parties.)

Tyranny of the minority flows in one direction: Minoritarianism, Minority Rule, Autocracy, Authoritarianism, Fascism, Totalitarianism, and more. Whatever the brand, something is rotten in the state of Democracy.

Because of the Electoral College, twice in the last two decades the presidential candidate who got more votes lost the general election (thereby electing George W. Bush and Donald Trump). That's half of the presidents from 2000 to 2020, or one president per decade.

The 2021–2022 Congress was split 50-50 senators in each party, but those 50 Democratic senators represented 41.5 million more people than the 50 Republican senators. If trends continue through the year 2040, 70 percent of Americans will be represented by 30 senators, and 30 percent of Americans by 70 senators. If you're reading this in 2024, 2040 is as far away as 2008.

A cornerstone of our political system is that it is a representative democracy, built with the intent to protect individual and minority rights from the tyranny of the majority. However, over the past few decades, we've increasingly seen a numerical minority of the electorate strategically build and entrench their power so that they can exercise disproportionate control over our laws, regardless of what the majority of Americans want. The methods have evolved over the decades, but the goal remains the same.

FOR FACTS' SAKE:

2000: George W. Bush becomes president even though Al Gore won the popular vote by more than 500,000 votes.

2016: Donald Trump wins the presidency even though Hillary Clinton won the popular vote by over 2.8 million votes.[2]

Laws that Entrenched Minority Rule

★ ★ ★

An interplay among federal laws, actions by state legislatures, and Supreme Court decisions has slowly chipped away at the extent to which the electorate is proportionally represented by elected government. As is the pattern with structural inequality, attempts to consolidate power to advance unpopular policies have disproportionately (and intentionally) impacted communities of color by entrenching existing structural advantages (regardless of whether Democrats or Republicans are drawing the maps).[3] Below is a very simplified history of how our political system has evolved to intentionally include, or exclude, citizens from our democracy at various moments.

1812: The term "gerry-mander" was coined in the name of Massachusetts governor Elbridge Gerry, who was in office when the state's electoral districts were redrawn in a formation that resembled a salamander (people are so clever). This commenced decades of gerrymandering electoral districts to entrench power and partisanship.[4]

The first gerrymander.[5]

1870: The 15th Amendment extends the right to vote to Black men.

1920: The 19th Amendment extends the right to vote to women (though in practice, largely only to white women).

1965: The Voting Rights Act is passed, outlawing racial discrimination in elections and requiring federal approval for certain states to change their voting laws.

1971: The Federal Election Campaign Act is passed to create limits on campaign spending.

1976: *Buckley v. Valeo.* The Supreme Court rules that political spending is speech and can't be restricted. Money wins.

2010: *Citizens United v. FEC.* The Supreme Court rules that it's unconstitutional to place any limits on independent expenditures for political campaigns by corporations, unions, and others. Money wins again.

2013: *Shelby County v. Holder.* The Supreme Court weakens the Voting Rights Act by overturning the section that required states that have a history of voting discrimination to get federal clearance when they change their election laws.

Money and Politics

* ★ *

One of the things we hear most often when we ask people why they've disengaged from politics is the argument that money controls the entire political process and that there's nothing us normies can do to change things. We happen to agree on the first part; the influence of money in politics isn't just a salient subplot in *Succession*. If anything, *Succession* is dangerously close to a documentary.

One of the driving forces behind money's influence on elected officials is quite simply that elections get longer and more expensive every year, and the constant fundraising cycle leaves officials open to undue influence from special interests whose donations they need, if not fully open to some light bribery on occasion.* Members of the House of Representatives need to raise money for reelection every two years (indeed, we've seen engagements last longer than Madison Cawthorn's tenure), and incumbents typically know about how many millions they'll need to make that happen, plus already have an existing roster of donors ready to deliver.

One of the biggest threats to democracy, though, is dark money. Dark money refers to political donations intended to influence elections made via nonprofit organizations, which are not required to disclose the identities of their donors. This was taken to a new level

---

* See: Secretary of the Interior Albert Bacon Fall of the Teapot Dome scandal (1921); Former Illinois governor Rod Blagojevich attempting to sell Barack Obama's vacant Senate seat after his 2008 election; former California representative Duke Cunningham attempting to trade military contracts for real estate (2005); lobbyist Jack Abramoff defrauding Native American tribes that were attempting to develop casinos on their reservations (2005). No shortage of names.

in 2013, when the Supreme Court's ruling in *Citizens United* opened the floodgates for unlimited dark money donations to legally enter the electoral system. Untraceable money can now be funneled into super PACs that are allowed to spend unlimited amounts of cash on any election, as long as it's not coordinated with a campaign.

Solutions to the Dark Money Problem

★ ★ ★

Naturally, people who oppose the *Citizens United* ruling aren't just going to let it lie. Some solutions have been proposed to increase transparency into who's making these bottomless political donations (so then we can figure out why they would care to do this when they could be buying snowmobiles and sushi instead).

The DISCLOSE Act: DISCLOSE stands for Democracy Is Strengthened by Casting Light on Spending in Elections . . . of course. First introduced in 2010, this legislation seeks to increase disclosure requirements for organizations that spend money in federal elections. Multiple sessions of Congress have attempted to pass this simple bill (is it *so* crazy to ask whose money this is?), but repeated efforts have failed. It could've celebrated its bar mitzvah by now.

State Disclosure Laws: Some states, such as California and Montana, have implemented their own disclosure laws targeting dark money. These require organizations to reveal their donors if they spend over a certain amount on state elections.

Federal Agencies: Some officials have called for reforms within the Federal Election Commission (FEC) or Internal Revenue Service (IRS) to better oversee and regulate organizations involved in political spending. You can see how that's been going.

Public Financing Options: More than 30 states and local governments have implemented public financing options for their elections, such as Arizona, Connecticut, Maine, and Michigan, as have New York City, Seattle, Albuquerque, Washington, D.C., and Montgomery County, Maryland.

So You Wanna Run for Office Without Dark Money Donors?

* ⭐ *

Alternatively, for those elected officials who would very much like to be excluded from this narrative, some will declare that their campaigns aren't accepting super PAC funding or contributions from corporations, and will fund their campaigns exclusively on small-dollar and individual donations.

While this is absolutely a great way to not have your vote bought, we'll note that this is an easier pledge for a candidate to make if their seat is "safe" due to their preexisting state or local demographics or gerrymandering, or when someone has vast personal wealth to self-fund a campaign.

When reading about big intractable issues like dark money and minority rule, it can feel like the deck is wholly stacked against us, but we don't want you to push your head further into the sand—and we think the rest of this book will convince you that you don't want to either. Many of the conversations that get the most attention in "the discourse" aren't the ones most people want solved. We don't care which bathroom the green M&M can use, we care about not getting shot at the grocery store. Our present rhetorical environment is pushing people into apathy and disengagement, further cementing policies that most of us don't support. Minority rule functions like credit card debt: a system that's set up to make it impossible to escape, because once you're in it, the advantages tend to compound to the party with power faster than the disadvantaged party can counter them.

American democracy has always had fundamental shortcomings. Yet even with its chapters of tremendous horror, there is no system that has brought more freedoms and prosperity to more citizens in human history than democracy. And it's undeniable that there has been substantial progress. To us, this is a system worth saving and improving—and we definitely believe that's still possible.

It's our right and privilege to keep fighting within this system to make life better, safer, and healthier for all Americans. With robust engagement and a more active electorate, we're certain that it's possible to bring the changes we want from within our democracy—flawed as it is—and that there's no better or more realistic option for Americans than to engage at scale and push for its fullest, most representative potential.

Polarized, Calcified, and Exhausted

AMERICANS ARE BURNT OUT. It's inevitable when every moment seems to bring a new set of unprecedented events. Who wants *more* political communication besides, well, politicians?

Even as two people who have a genuine (and yes, idealistic) interest in politics, we know that it calls to mind:

1. A loud and performative battle of egos between eternal incumbents who care more about their own power than the people who elected them;

2. Facts being twisted so far that they are unrecognizable; poorly made frog memes that push conspiracies and disinformation, funded by who the hell knows; and

3. Relatively little clarity on the real source or truth of many widespread claims.

For some, politics has caused immense personal pain. Family members no longer speak because their political beliefs have become an unbridgeable gulf. And then there is the pain that results from active policymaking decisions (for example, cutting regulations on

SAMI SAGE & EMILY AMICK

air and water for the sake of juicing corporate profits, rolling back antidiscrimination laws, the refusal to pass widely favored legislation such as universal background checks for gun purchasers, to name a few).

Despite experiencing the isolation of a global pandemic and watching an insurrection unfold live on our small, medium, and large screens, there has been no moment of national catharsis or movement toward restoring the faith of the electorate. Instead, the polarization has crystallized, and our information sources have diverged even further.

There are three political science terms that are often used to describe this feeling of intense stratification: polarization, tribalization, and calcification.

Polarization is the widening divide between political ideologies and the scarcity of shared values among opposing groups. Tribalization is the formation of distinct political tribes or groups that share common values, ideologies, and strong internal loyalty. These political identities then seep into our social and cultural life. Lilliana Mason, a political science professor at Johns Hopkins University, has extensively studied this trend, describing how political conflicts integrate into social identities, resulting in fervent group loyalty.[6] Calcification is the process of hardening and entrenching political beliefs, making them more resistant to change.

These three trends have profoundly shaped the political landscape—both how it functions (worse than ever) and how we experience it. Research has found what we know instinctively: increased polarization contributes to gridlock and prevents the passage of bipartisan legislation that would typically help *all of us*. (In 2023 Congress passed 27 bills that became law. Usually it passes hundreds.)[7] It can also breed an environment of hostility, further anchoring party loyalties.

Tribalization intensifies political divisions by forming closely knit groups that view outsiders with suspicion or even hostility. Mason's work also emphasizes how this can diminish empathy and common understanding between different political groups, thereby stifling productive dialogue. When this tribalization then becomes calcified, it reinforces in on itself with individuals interacting only with people who hold similar views, leading to even more extreme opinions. And that's how Taylor Swift became a Democratic psyop asset.

These trends have been amplified by our modern media ecosystem. When you're looking for a show to watch or scrolling your feed, what catches your eye? For a lot of people, it ends up being the voices that stir emotions and validate their already held beliefs. There is a dual desire to be outraged and validated that pushes creators to provoke cycles of anger, urgency, and blame. In today's modern media environment, everything from Fox News to YouTube's rabbit hole, algorithms incentivize the type of emotional hyperbole that captures people's attention, with total disregard for the long-term consequences.

> "We get to a point where the exhaustion is itself exhausting. And I firmly believe that the forces who seek to undermine our society, who seek to pit us against each other for their cynical gain, see exhaustion as a potent weapon at their disposal."
>
> —DAN RATHER

In 2018, a group of researchers at an organization called More In Common launched a project called The Hidden Tribes of America to study polarization.[8] They surveyed people about their core beliefs and basic values, and based on the data, identified seven distinct political groups in the U.S. The "tribes of America," according to the report, are: progressive activists (8 percent), traditional liberals (11 percent), passive liberals (15 percent), politically disengaged (26 percent), moderates (15 percent), traditional conservatives (19 percent), and devoted conservatives (6 percent). But their most critical finding was that four out of the seven groups, which total 67 percent of Americans, fit within a broader category that they titled the "Exhausted Majority" whose views fall somewhere in the middle.

While one might assume this means the people who fall into that category hold moderate or centrist beliefs, that was not actually their finding. Rather, the main characteristic that bound this group was their rejection of political polarization and extremism. Ideologically, they hold a diversity of views that are flexible on various issues but are all united by their frustration with the extremes, exclusion from public discourse, and their shared interest in finding common ground. The Exhausteds are a mix of traditional and passive liberals, moderates, and those who are politically disengaged.

By their very nature of being exhausted by the political discourse, this isn't a loud group of people, which is a very different tune than the one we typically hear when it comes to political discourse. The project found that only one group on the left (progressive activists) and two on the right (traditional and devoted conservatives)

"I simultaneously want to stick my head so far deep in the sand and run away from the awful of it all AND save the world for myself and my children. So I feel guilty for not doing more, ashamed about the current state, and overwhelmed about what to do with all that."

—Amanda, age 35, Bethesda, Maryland

"I'm fighting the feeling of apathy and discouragement constantly. It's hard to remain optimistic when the general consensus says one thing but what actually happens is vastly different (ahem, popular vote vs. Electoral College)."

—Jennifer, age 35, Gresham, Oregon

"I feel like it's nearly impossible to have a calm, nuanced, normal conversation about many policy issues or politicians. I feel like people can't see past the misinformation or hatred and aren't interested in learning. Not all people— I have found many online who I find helpful and hopeful. But in person, especially where I live, it's extremely difficult."

—Sarah, age 41, Kalispell, Montana

"I feel like most of our current politicians (up and down the ballot) are too busy fighting each other instead of doing the work."

—Jamie, age 38, New Albany, Indiana

"I feel frustrated most frequently. In my youth, I was idealistic and assumed that people who were interested in running for office did so because they wanted to serve their communities. I suppose I took things at face value when I started learning about government and civil servants. However, as I have started paying more attention, I get increasingly frustrated that there are so many representatives who choose to only serve the interests of a select few people."

—Amanda, age 33, Atlanta, Georgia

FOR FACTS' SAKE:

Below are several examples of policies that most Americans agree on.

Gun Violence: 9 out of 10 Americans support background checks for gun sales,[9] and 77 percent of Americans support red flag laws that would allow a family member to petition a court to remove someone's guns when they are a threat to themselves or others.[10]

Voting Rights: Most Americans support "no excuse" voting, including that you should be able to vote by mail, early, or absentee without an excuse,[11] and two thirds of Americans support creating a federal holiday for voting in federal elections.[12]

Abortion: 61 percent of U.S. adults say that abortion should be legal in all or most cases.[13]

LGBTQ+ rights: 80 percent of Americans favor laws that protect LGBTQ+ people from discrimination in jobs, public accommodations, and housing.[14] Only 10 percent of Americans oppose laws that would protect trans people from discrimination.[15]

Climate Change: Two thirds of Americans support prioritizing renewable energy sources, and the main group in opposition is conservatives over age 65.[16]

hold strident, often morality-based views, and those groups tend to monopolize conversations in the media and online.

These findings shouldn't be interpreted to mean that there isn't a role for the wings of the political parties (when those wings are not based in racism/violence/denial of facts), or that those who hold those views in earnest are any less important than those somewhere in the vast middle. In fact, it is often those groups that change the moral fabric of America (marriage equality and abortion access are examples where advocates achieved legislative and constitutional changes that affect all of us).

However, public discourse tends to over-index on content from the groups on the wings. Whether and how they assert power over policymaking is a more complicated question. We are talking vibes, and while the vibes may be loud, they are not reflective of this vast Exhausted Majority, representing two thirds of the country.

As polarized and antagonistic as our culture feels right now, we can work to avoid a self-fulfilling prophecy by turning the vibes around. A recent study from the Institute of Labor Economics analyzed public writing and rhetoric across multiple periods and found that the mood of a society directly correlates with social progress and economic conditions.[17]

While election results and passing legislation depend on cold, hard numbers, what's behind those numbers often reflects how people are *feeling* about our country, which is somewhat a phenomenon of mass psychology. Mass sentiment is driven by a whole set of factors, often based on the media we consume, the people we surround ourselves with (and their views), our preexisting ideologies, and our personal circumstances. According to a 2021 peer-reviewed study in the *Proceedings of the National Academy of Sciences*, facts are not as convincing in political arguments as personal anecdotes are.[18] While there is certainly a place for storytelling in political messaging, the total abandonment of facts in favor of emotional arguments has kept us stuck in a vicious cycle.

The more Exhausteds disengage from the system, the more the system's vibes become extreme, the further the Exhausteds are pushed out. But we hope you will look at this another way: there's potential. While the vibes are bad and polarized, as you can see in the For Facts' Sake box on the previous page, the numbers are not.

Hope and inspiration can be hard to channel, and though it may sound naïve, there is a practical need to cultivate hope, joy, and inspiration above the noise. Engaging with toxic commentary, even to refute it, can help amplify it, so try to save your energy for conversations and actions that might make a difference. Americans agree over more than we assume, and if we work to build coalitions around our commonalities, there is so much potential for change and, dare we say, even reasons to be optimistic.

Hopelessness Is a Civic Engagement Killer

IF WE COULD SOMEHOW attend a national group therapy session, we think the therapist would say that our collective outrage and cynicism are covering up a secondary emotion: hopelessness.

It's a logical endpoint to years, decades (!) of political and social change, and being hammered by interests that benefit from our apathy. In President Obama's speech at the 2020 Democratic National Convention, he emphasized that the people in power count on it, arguing that they know they "can't win you over with their policies" and so they try to convince you that your vote doesn't matter, and that participating in taking away their power is pointless. "That's how they get to keep making decisions that affect your life, and the lives of the people you love."

Recognizing the hopelessness spiral is the first step toward getting out of it.

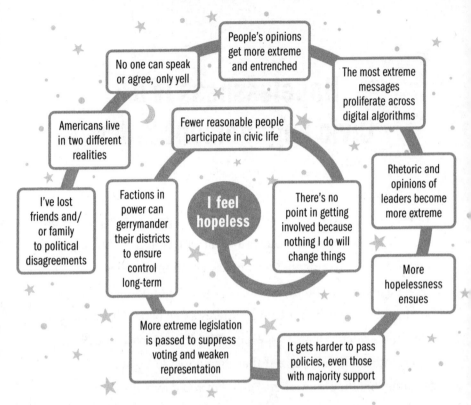

The Hopelessness Spiral

Hopelessness can be addictive, especially when our phones feed us constant evidence that confirms our pessimism and cynicism. In a world full of painful events that our phones dutifully keep us informed about, at least it feels good to be right about how bad things are. In recent years, psychologists have noted that doom-scrolling is affecting people's mental health and they're "perseverating on it."[1] And by that five-dollar word, they mean to continue thinking about it long after the interaction is over—an inability to move on. As Harvard Law School professor Cass Sunstein observed,

"When people talk to like-minded others, they tend to amplify their preexisting views, end up in a more extreme position, dismiss other positions . . . and become more confident and unified."[2] This is exactly the dynamic of how online echo chambers can drive and reinforce hopelessness.

If you're in the early phases of doomscrolling withdrawal, you may not be prepared for this next step, but we'll throw it out there anyway. Activist and educator Mariame Kaba, whose work focuses on (among other things) violence in the prison-industrial complex, has popularized her teaching that hope is a discipline. It's not a fuzzy feeling that a happy ending is inevitably on its way; neither is it an emotion, nor a sense of optimism.

> "I'm telling you there is hope. I have seen it, but it does not come from the governments or corporations. It comes from the people."
>
> —GRETA THUNBERG

Hope is a practice that requires us to continuously choose to look within ourselves and our communities for answers, while also creating boundaries that permit us to have unspoiled moments and spaces for joy. We can reverse a hopelessness spiral through the compounding and life-affirming effects of empathy, togetherness, and community.

The next section discusses how you can throw a wrench into the destructive spiral of hopelessness, but first, we want to delve into your hope outlook.

What Is Your Hope Outlook?

* ⭐ *

A lot of self-help books call on you to change. We're not here to do that—we love you for you (even if that's a pessimist 90 percent of the time), but our goal is to help you find a way to channel your natural tendencies into productive action. Regardless of whether you're hopeless or hopeful—we think it's helpful to know your "hope outlook" (a phrase we're using to describe your instinctive mindset toward the future). Obviously, we aren't cup of water girlies; it's iced coffee or bust:

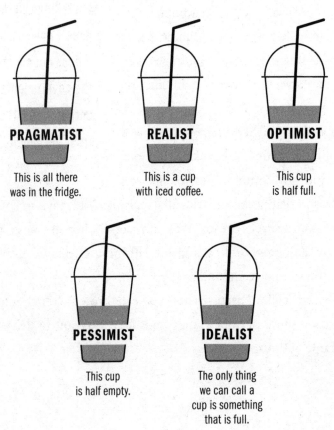

PRAGMATIST
This is all there
was in the fridge.

REALIST
This is a cup
with iced coffee.

OPTIMIST
This cup
is half full.

PESSIMIST
This cup
is half empty.

IDEALIST
The only thing
we can call a
cup is something
that is full.

PRAGMATIST

For people with a pragmatic hope outlook, it is what it is, and we work with what we have. A pragmatist is focused on practical solutions to problems, and they prioritize outcomes over theoretical ideals. They're problem solvers who rely on empirical evidence of what's possible, instead of how the possibilities match their ideological hopes and dreams.

✶ ✶ ★ A PRAGMATIST SOUNDS LIKE . . . ★ ✶ ✶

"I find engaging with political news and environments equal parts exciting and exhausting. Exciting because I feel like I finally understand the civic sphere and my realm of influence. I have been able to plug into several local organizations and exert my voice, beyond just voting, for the first time in my life. Due to some amazing Instagram accounts and my county party's leaders, I now know what bills are being considered and passed on the state level, I know what my City Council is voting on, and I know who to contact to tell my appreciation and/or opposition. This makes me feel so much better than simply rage sharing when my representatives do something ridiculous."
—Kristen, age 34, Shawnee, Kansas

Are You a Pragmatist?

▷ In a group project, are you typically the one who brings conversations back to the practical steps that need to get done?

▷ Do you find yourself naturally assessing the pros and cons of a situation before taking a stand on it?

▶ Do you believe that perfect should not be the enemy of the good when making decisions?

▶ Are you skeptical of grand plans?

Emily: *This is me 100 percent. I'm always a rat in a maze looking for an exit. This often annoys people because I'm not one to sit in frustration and talk about problems. I also focus on solutions that are attainable rather than ideal. For me, progress is better than perfection.*

Pragmatists in Community:

▶ As a pragmatist, you are the one who does things like figuring out how to get speed bumps added to your street. Sometimes it can be hard when other people want to talk about their hopes and dreams and not *the plan.*

▶ Your biggest allies will be realists; they are sitting in the same brass-tacks world as you. They can help you understand the lay of the land, and then it's your time to shine to figure out a path to progress.

▶ Take time to listen to the idealists and optimists; sometimes you can lose the forest for the trees and forget the "why" behind the work you are doing. They are the ones who can ground you in purpose and reveal creative options.

▶ Pessimists can help you refine your vision and prepare for what (to you) will be unexpected bumps in the road. This will make you more prepared and in control of what lies ahead.

Hope Shift Tips:

Celebrate Small Victories: Focus on the incremental progress you can make. Each step forward is a piece of a larger puzzle and can build momentum toward progress.

Strategic Planning: Create a roadmap of actionable steps toward your goals. Seeing a clear path can renew your sense of hope.

REALIST

This is the hope outlook that's embodied by someone who sees the world as it is, not as they wish it to be. Not that they don't have their own wishes for how it should be, but in practical situations, they tend to prioritize understanding and reacting to the current circumstances and are often skeptical of ideologically led approaches.

* * ★ **A REALIST SOUNDS LIKE . . .** ★ * *

"I remind myself that the news gets paid more for pissing me off and I cut out the inflammatory news sources when possible. I also take breaks from time to time so I can come back more engaged and action focused instead of complaint focused."

—Allyson, age 37, Troy, Michigan

Are You a Realist?

▶ In conversation, do you find yourself cautioning others about the limitations of grand ideas?

▶ Are you the one who tends to mention the unintended consequences of well-meaning actions in complex systems?

▶ Do you think that acknowledging the harsh truths about something is essential for improving it?

▶ Do you think that working within an existing system is the best way to get things done?

Sami: *Emily says I'm a realist (how pragmatic of her to want a clear answer), though I can think of times in my life when I've displayed qualities of all the hope outlooks. I've found this framework to be especially helpful when thinking about how to communicate with people—looking at things from their hope outlook helps me understand their concerns and priorities.*

Realists in Community:

▶ As a realist, you are capable of assessing a situation and seeing it for what it is, warts and all. But it means you also have a tendency to doom spiral if you can't see a way out of the current predicament.

▸ Pragmatists are your best buddy because they can help you plan a path forward. Optimists and, especially, idealists can frustrate you because it feels like they aren't willing to face reality.

▸ Sometimes your frank view of the system means you think the only way to get through it is to chuck the whole thing out the window—the pessimists will be with you on that.

Hope Shift Tips:

Gratitude: Catalogue aspects of your life or community that are functioning well. Gratitude for what's working can be a foundation for hope.

Knowledge as Power: Arm yourself with knowledge about the issues you care about. Understanding the nuances can make the path toward improvement clearer and more hopeful.

OPTIMIST

An optimist is someone who innately believes things are bound to improve, that most (if not all) people are inherently good, even in the face of much evidence to the contrary. They focus on the positive potential in people and situations rather than dwelling on the current negatives. It's possible to be optimistic (or pessimistic) while simultaneously being a realist, pragmatist, or idealist.

"I feel excited to politically and civically engage as much as I can. The world feels dark, and engaging with peers about what is going on helps me to feel less hopeless and more hopeful. I really enjoy listening and talking with friends about their concerns and what issues matter to them most."

—Kate, age 38, New York

Are You an Optimist?

▶ When you hear about a setback or failure, do you tend to underestimate how bad it will be?

▶ Do you often find yourself reassuring others that things will get better?

▶ When facing criticism or pessimism, do you naturally respond with counterarguments that emphasize hope and resilience?

▶ Do you actively seek out and share stories that illustrate human kindness, progress, or breakthroughs, even when such stories are rare or overlooked by others?

Optimists in Community:

▶ As an optimist, you are the heart and soul of all the things (your family, your PTA, your friend's campaign) but it also means you often feel private disappointment when things don't turn out how you hoped.

▸ A realist helps ground you in what's happening, and they can give you the quick download on the 411 that you don't have the bandwidth to learn yourself.

▸ Pessimists are hard for you to handle, so protecting your spirit is something important to take time for.

Hope Shift Tips:

Embrace a Growth Mindset: View challenges as opportunities for growth. This perspective can transform barriers into sources of hope.

Share Your Optimism: Actively spread your hopeful perspective to others. Optimism can be infectious, and reinforcing it through sharing can strengthen it within you.

PESSIMIST

These are the people who consistently expect the worst. These Eeyores are the ones who focus on the limitations and flaws within a system and of human nature, often doubting the potential for significant positive change. They are innate skeptics, ready with a list of cons, and it takes a great deal to gain their trust, if even possible.

⋆ ⋆ ⋆ **A PESSIMIST SOUNDS LIKE . . .** ⋆ ⋆ ⋆

"How do we get out of this mess? How can we get out of this system where it feels like nothing can get done because the two main parties seem to be moving further apart?"
—Alexis, age 32, Wichita, Kansas

Are You a Pessimist?

▸ When you hear about a new initiative or policy, is your first reaction to question its feasibility or ability to actually fix anything?

▸ Are you skeptical that large-scale positive change is possible?

▸ Are you frequently deterred from taking action that you feel isn't worth it?

▸ Do you believe that the flaws of human nature limit the efficacy of government and political systems?

Pessimists in Community:

▸ As a pessimist we are frankly shocked you are reading this book. Thank you.

▸ There's comfort in expecting the worst and getting pleasantly surprised when things go better than you expected, so this can be your superpower to help you stay engaged in the political process when others want to tap out.

▸ Pessimism and cynicism go hand in hand but are not the same. What's important is to find people who help you see the possibilities. Pragmatists, realists, and idealists are good intellectual sparring partners to keep you from spiraling.

Hope Shift Tips *(a couple extra for you . . .):*

Make a Risk Assessment: Recognize that expecting the worst can be a form of emotional risk management. Understanding this can help you gradually open up to a more positive outlook.

Find Reliable Allies: Build relationships with those who have a track record of reliability. Trustworthy connections can provide a foundation for cautious hope.

Document Progress: Keep a journal or log of times when outcomes were better than expected. Reflecting on these can challenge your preconceived notions.

Celebrate Surprises: When things turn out better than expected, take time to celebrate. Recognizing these moments can slowly shift your perspective.

Engage in Constructive Criticism: Use your critical eye to identify potential improvements rather than just flaws. This can turn skepticism into a tool for fostering hope.

IDEALIST

An idealist is someone who prioritizes ideology and moral principles above all else, even to their own detriment at times. They are driven by their values and beliefs and want to make the world a better place in accordance with their vision. They tend to have an interesting mix of optimism (that they'll one day be able to achieve this) and pessimism (about the status quo).

"Look at my kids—I can't stop fighting for them. Even when shit gets tough or when I feel defeated. I think that I'm lucky to get to fight for kids who are still here living on this earth because the reality is too many parents are fighting a fight that has already cost them everything."

—Cory, age 39, Tomball, Texas

Are You an Idealist?

▶ Do you feel a responsibility to elevate conversations to discuss "what should be" rather than "what is"?

▶ When considering social change, do you place greater value on the intention behind actions rather than the practical outcomes?

▶ Are you drawn to visions of a more perfect society?

▶ Do you often find yourself advocating for changes that align with your sense of justice, even if they're not practical or popular?

Idealists in Community:

▶ As an idealist you are very focused on how it should be—you live in the future. It can be overwhelming to figure out how to get from here to there, and this can make you want to tap out.

▶ Optimists are your bestie for helping you buttress your belief that change is possible; they can help animate your spirit in a way that others can't.

▸ An idealist/pessimist pairing (aka: golden retriever/ black cat) is iconic. These two opposites balance each other out and find an absurdist joy in the other.

▸ Pragmatists probably annoy you; it's fine—they are annoying.

Hope Shift Tips:

Identify Hope Anchors: Identify specific moments in your life when you've been validated in your hopefulness. You can use this to anchor your mindset when you get pulled into a hopelessness spiral.

Connect with Inspirational Stories: Seek out narratives of individuals or movements that have stayed true to their ideals and achieved change. This can reinforce the power of idealism.

Reflection Exercise

BEFORE WE HEAD INTO the next section of the book, we want to ask you to take a moment to go deep into your feelings.

TAKE STOCK OF YOURSELF:

▸ On a scale of 1–10, how would you rate your level of hopelessness?

▸ What three words would you use to describe how you *feel* about politics? Do you feel differently about community or civic life?

▸ How do you see those two as distinct?

▸ Do you think that negative feelings often overwhelm your ability to consume political news or participate in civic life?

"Hope is a discipline."

—MARIAME KABA

Short journaling exercise: Write out a rant on the political issue you feel is the most hopeless. (Don't be self-conscious about your rage. The purpose of the exercise is to write how you feel, translated from your internal dialogue.)

Now consider the issue you just journaled about through the lens of each of the five hope outlooks. Write down one to two sentences encapsulating how each outlook would view the prospect of changing the issue you feel hopeless about.

_____

_____

_____

_____

_____

_____

_____

_____

_____

_____

_____

_____

_____

_____

_____

_____

_____

_____

_____

_____

Take at least a 15-minute break, then come back and reflect on the issue again. Use this space to journal any reflections on the issue you were hopeless about, and notice any emotional shifts and/or thoughts and feelings about the five hope outlooks.

When you finish this exercise, go to page 180, "Bringing It All Together," and write down a few notes.

SECTION 3:
SO, WHAT CAN WE DO?

Action Is the Antidote to Despair

MANY OF US WERE TAUGHT from a young age that "politics" is a topic that comes with restrictions. Not at the dinner table. Not in polite conversation. Not when you first meet someone. The lesson, especially for women, was that it's best we don't broach subjects that might rock the boat, make people uncomfortable, or cause disagreement. It can also be legitimately uncomfortable to discuss, especially in situations where differing opinions are also reflective of unequal power dynamics or can have real consequences for personal relationships.

Who benefits from normalized silence on politics? Or anything for that matter? If your opinion didn't have power, there would be no effort made to shut you up.

The most effective methodology for getting out the vote is something called "relational organizing," which is really just . . . talking about politics to people you know. Texting between friends increased voting by 8 percent in the 2018 midterms, according to a study published by the Columbia University Data Science Institute.[1] It's also proven to be an effective tool for rapid public health response and building community partnerships.[2]

SAMI SAGE & EMILY AMICK

Silence on politics is also a contributing factor to our polarized political landscape—and conversely having conversations about it is a part of the solution. Research has shown that talking about politics is a key tactic in building consensus. A study by social neurologist Beau Sievers, who is currently a research scientist at the Stanford Social Neuroscience Laboratory, found that robust conversations that result in consensus actually change people's brains. In other words, the feeling of "clicking" with someone is a quantifiable phenomenon.

"Action is the antidote to despair."

—JOAN BAEZ

It may seem that only those already in power are the ones with the ability to make change, but democracy is a participation sport, and if we all take on one small part, we can make big changes.

The goal of a rich civic life isn't one in which every conversation is a battle that overwhelms you. For political action to be sustainable for most people, it has to provide some moments of joy, fulfillment, community, and purpose. What if our political mindset were rooted in inspiration instead of despair? Before we take action, we need to envision a better future for ourselves, our kids, and our communities.

Why Action Is the Antidote to Despair

* ★ *

1. It may appear that our institutions are immutable, but the pulleys and levers of government are supposed to be controlled by us (the voters). We can influence, pressure, and if need be, replace the decision-makers. Your calls to Congress, your social media posts, your votes, and your real-life conversations make a difference.

2. Each of us does not need to shoulder the full responsibility of changing the world, but all of us each doing the small things we are individually equipped and motivated to do can create sweeping long-term change.

3. Talking about things you're worried about is an important part of solving them, while refusing to engage with our country's very real challenges is a glidepath for extremists to attain power. The purpose of talking about politics is to come together and find solutions. Talking (constructively and in good faith) is a form of action.

4. It's long been said that decisions are made by those who show up, and nowhere is that truer than with governing. Naturally, those who hold the most extreme views and the strongest incentives to maintain power are going to show up the most regularly—they're the ones who are willing to dedicate their lives to a cause and use their money and energy to make their singular policy

dream come true. (See, also, corporations that can pay people to make it their full-time jobs.) For the rest of us, politics will only ever be one piece of our life—though it can fill many voids that you probably haven't thought of, like finding new friendships in your community.

5. Working closely with people who share your values will give you a sense of purpose and possibility in a way that nothing else does. You will experience challenges and disappointments in the process, but then you will see the potential you have to change people's lives for the better—and once you get a taste of that you won't ever want to give it up.

For civic action to be sufficiently meaningful it needs to be rooted in your values. So, as we dive into the action-planning section of the book, we ask you to start with a (somewhat lengthy) exercise aimed at helping you drill down on your core values.

Developing Your Personal Mission Statement

IN ITS PUREST FORM, "politics" is a catchall term to describe the way individuals and communities translate their values into an operational government. But if you ask anyone with a busy civic life what motivates them—even if you were to ask the most craven politician you can think of—nearly all of them would cite the desire to make a positive difference in people's lives. How one defines "positive" has been debated since Adam, but the broader point is that fulfillment from civic engagement comes from seeing your values reflected in the rules and norms that govern your community.

Values provide a meeting point for you and others who share them. They influence how we interact with our family, friends, and neighbors; the careers we pursue; how we spend our free time; and how we save and spend money, and on what. If someone says they want to do something and they have nothing stopping them, but still aren't doing that thing, that could signal how much they truly value that thing. Clarifying what you care about and focusing on it keeps you authentic, consistent, and motivated.

Your values are not static. As you evolve and your circumstances change, it's possible your values may shift, too. This exercise aims to help you learn more about yourself. The goal isn't to be prescriptive, but to check in with yourself. The same way an organization devises its mission statement, having a few core values statements will help you develop an approach to civic engagement that is authentic, meaningful, and fulfilling for you. Our goal is to empower you to find a way to weave civic engagement into your everyday life in a sustainable way, however that looks. We suggest going back and thinking about your answers to the prior two reflection exercises and what major themes you can take away from those answers. Do this in whatever way is the best fit for your brain, whether that means writing it down by free association or talking about it with your friends, your partner, your family, or anyone else whose opinion you respect. Make a vision board if you like crafting.

No grades and no gold stars are forthcoming (apologies to the eldest daughters), so if you don't know your answers immediately, let it marinate. Even if you know your answers, still let it marinate. Bring it up with your therapist. Hopefully, the following questions will be revealing and helpful.

1. Who are the people you care most about in the world?

2. What are the most important things you hope to provide for those you care about?

3. How would you describe the ideal town for you to live in?

_____
_____
_____
_____
_____
_____
_____
_____

4. Think about the people in your life you admire and whose values you aspire to share. How would you describe them? What values do they hold that you admire?

_____
_____
_____
_____
_____
_____
_____
_____

5. Write out a list of the political issues you care about most. For each issue, write out:

▶ Why is this important to you?

▶ What caused you to care about this first?

▶ Who, or what parties, benefit from maintaining the status quo?

_____

_____

_____

_____

_____

_____

_____

_____

_____

_____

_____

_____

_____

_____

_____

_____

_____

_____

_____

6. Word choice exercise. Quickly scan through this list and circle all the words you feel reflect who you are. What values are most core to your identity?

Responsibility Friendship Intuition Integrity Generosity

Boldness Pride Kindness Thoughtfulness Sensibility

Solidarity Cooperation Respect Justice Understanding

Nurture Freedom Stewardship Trust Morality

Outspokenness Authenticity Persistence Compassion Truth

Empathy Equity Risk-taking Belonging Power

Vulnerability Transparency Adaptability Strength Inclusivity

Fairness Bravery Sincerity Leisure Intentionality

Tenacity Diversity Security Inclusion Fortitude

Discipline Curiosity Service Connection Recognition

Gratitude Honestly Competency Tradition Collaboration

Grit Safety Joy Liberation Balance

Community Intelligence Courage Benevolence Interdependency

Knowledge Competence Initiative Heritage Rest

Loyalty Creativity Harmony Charity Reliability

Resilience Logic Support Accountability Openness

Simplicity Humility Growth Resourcefulness Altruism

Passion Reasonableness Patriotism Stewardship Faith

Self-discipline Self-determination Pragmatism Optimism

7. Write down all the words you circled, grouping similar values together.

8. Reread your answers to questions 2–5 and pull out the values that are most important to you. What makes you feel excited, even if you're not quite sure why? What do you want to talk about with your friends? What feels like they are part of who you are/how you define yourself? Use the words you chose in question 7 as a starting point. (Example: I care about education, and I want all kids to have a *fair* chance at life.)

9. Group all your values into three themes and identify the word in each group that represents the core value.

10. Write out a values statement with each of the three words you identified in the previous question, followed by one sentence describing why this is important to you. When you read this statement, you should feel energized to make these values a reality. These words should embody the purpose that underlies your daily actions, your hopes, and what you are working toward. (Example: I value fairness, because I want all children to have the education, healthcare, and full stomachs to succeed. I value trust, because I want to feel united with my neighbors and part of a community that works together.)

11. Look over your values statements and consider some of the following questions:

- How do these values shape your political decisions?

- How do your values connect you to your community?

- What do you do when values clash?

- Have your values changed over time? How?

- How can understanding your values help you build bridges with those around you?

_____
_____
_____
_____
_____
_____
_____
_____
_____
_____
_____
_____
_____
_____
_____
_____
_____
_____
_____
_____
_____

When you finish this exercise, go to page 180,
"Bringing It All Together," and write down a few notes.

SECTION 4:
YOUR CIVIC PERSONALITY

What Is a Civic Personality?

IF WE'RE GOING TO HAVE any shot at achieving a less polarized, more civically engaged, and legitimately representative democracy, we need people to rediscover the purpose and enjoyment in civic life. For this to be sustainable, it needs to be authentic to who you are. The work itself, unpaid labor on top of all the other stuff you do in your day-to-day life, should feel like an extension of your true self *and* an extension of the values you want to live. You need to feel like you have found a place in your community where you belong and look forward to it more than you don't. Fill-your-cup stuff. Research has long established that humans have a universal need to belong, and that fulfilling this need has positive psychological outcomes.[1] We tend to repeat things that make us feel good, so we want to help you figure out what that thing (or things) could be for you.

We proffer* four categories of civic personalities (Leaders, Givers, Connectors, and Creators), but they aren't meant to be rigid molds. You could fall into more than one, and it may even change during different seasons of your life. Our goal is to help you explore

---

* "To offer for acceptance." An annoying word used by lawyers, when they could just use *offer*. See also: *use* versus *utilize*.

SAMI SAGE & EMILY AMICK

how your personality, skills, and interests can intersect to contribute to your community.

The journey of discovering our civic personality is rooted in self-reflection, introspection, and an understanding of our values and aspirations. It's an invitation to explore your passions and talents, to consider the issues that resonate deeply with you, and to find meaningful and creative ways to give back. It's an opportunity to embrace your individuality while recognizing our shared commitment to building a better society.

If you're following the light parallels to astrology, consider these groupings to be comparable to the concept of fire, earth, water, and air signs, and how the signs within those groups share some common qualities.

Civic Personality Quiz

SOME OF US BOUGHT *Seventeen* for the horoscopes, others for the fashion advice, and some of us were there for the quizzes.

Go through each statement and mark how strongly you feel each sentiment applies (or doesn't) to you. Then come back and add up each column (1 point for every check in "Strongly Disagree," 2 points for every check in "Disagree," and so on), then find the total number of points per section. The section with the highest number of total points is your strongest civic personality.

(*Shortcut*: if you hate math—do the quiz and then just figure out what section has the most Agrees and Strongly Agrees.)

Strongly Disagree	Disagree	Neutral	Agree	Strongly Agree
①	②	③	④	⑤

★ ★ ★ SECTION 1 ★ ★ ★

	1	2	3	4	5
I possess a natural ability to read a room and intuit what drives people emotionally.	○	○	○	○	○
I believe that listening to others is as important as speaking, and I practice both with intent.	○	○	○	○	○
When I commit to a task, I follow through until it's completed.	○	○	○	○	○
I am unafraid to be bold and stand up for my beliefs, even if it means being labeled as "difficult."	○	○	○	○	○
I am often the first to voice my opinion in a group setting.	○	○	○	○	○
If something needs to get done, and no one is stepping up, I will.	○	○	○	○	○
I feel a surge of energy when I discuss a cause I am passionate about.	○	○	○	○	○
I can talk my way out of (almost) anything.	○	○	○	○	○
I often find myself thinking about the future and envisioning what can be improved.	○	○	○	○	○
I'm a planner, I love an itinerary.	○	○	○	○	○

TOTAL (add up each column): ___ ___ ___ ___ ___

TOTAL of all columns: _____

★ ★ ★ SECTION 2 ★ ★ ★

① ② ③ ④ ⑤

Completing a project gives me a
strong sense of accomplishment.

○ ○ ○ ○ ○

I don't follow the crowd; my actions are guided
by my internal compass of what feels right.

○ ○ ○ ○ ○

Practical solutions appeal to me
more than hypothetical ideas.

○ ○ ○ ○ ○

The well-being of those around me
is as vital to me as my own.

○ ○ ○ ○ ○

I'm an efficiency queen; I want things done
in the most practical way possible.

○ ○ ○ ○ ○

I am thoughtful and cautious; I want to
make sure the next step is the right one.

○ ○ ○ ○ ○

My friends call me when they are
going through a hard time.

○ ○ ○ ○ ○

I do not like being the center of attention.

○ ○ ○ ○ ○

I think actions are better than words.

○ ○ ○ ○ ○

I am extremely open to other people's
perspectives and take experiences
as they come.

○ ○ ○ ○ ○

TOTAL (add up each column): ___ ___ ___ ___ ___

TOTAL of all columns: _____

★ ★ ★ SECTION 3 ★ ★ ★

	1	2	3	4	5
I am a good explainer—even when something is confusing I can help others get to a place of understanding.	◯	◯	◯	◯	◯
I think everyone has something valuable to add to any situation.	◯	◯	◯	◯	◯
I frequently start conversations with strangers (e.g., in the coffee shop line).	◯	◯	◯	◯	◯
When friends or family are fighting, I'm often the one called on to help resolve it.	◯	◯	◯	◯	◯
I thrive more in collaboration than in competition.	◯	◯	◯	◯	◯
The best trips are ones that are spontaneous.	◯	◯	◯	◯	◯
I love hosting a dinner party, facilitating a group hang, or getting everyone to attend an event.	◯	◯	◯	◯	◯
I know many of my neighbors.	◯	◯	◯	◯	◯
I don't expect immediate results for things; I can wait.	◯	◯	◯	◯	◯
I consider gossiping to be one of my favorite hobbies.	◯	◯	◯	◯	◯

TOTAL (add up each column): ___ ___ ___ ___ ___

TOTAL of all columns: _____

★ ★ ★ SECTION 4 ★ ★ ★

	1	2	3	4	5
I feel energized when I connect with people on a deep level.	○	○	○	○	○
Creativity is my superpower.	○	○	○	○	○
I am a truth teller and think knowledge can be transformational.	○	○	○	○	○
I'm restless, but it propels me to new ideas and experiences.	○	○	○	○	○
I often challenge myself to find new perspectives and am not afraid to explore topics that are considered taboo.	○	○	○	○	○
I have a knack for expressing complex ideas in a way people can understand.	○	○	○	○	○
I value aesthetics and think art is a powerful medium for conversation.	○	○	○	○	○
I am always looking for patterns and connections between things.	○	○	○	○	○
I don't shy away from controversial topics.	○	○	○	○	○
I prioritize authenticity.	○	○	○	○	○

TOTAL (add up each column): ___ ___ ___ ___ ___

TOTAL of all columns: ___

TOTAL SCORE FOR EACH SECTION:

1. Leader: _____   3. Connector: _____

2. Giver: _____   4. Creator: _____

Leaders / FIRE

Summary

✦ ★ ✦

History shapes our idea of what makes a "leader." Yet the characteristics that many Americans typically associate with leaders of the past (e.g., strong, powerful, loud, male) don't reflect either (a) all the different types of people who are good leaders or (b) the actual qualities that make someone a good leader.

Maybe you've always been at the head of the line and have called yourself "the leader" since day 1 of kindergarten, or maybe you've never thought about yourself that way. Leadership doesn't need to mean running for President (though it can, President Barbie!); it means being the steady individual who can steer the ship to safety, to better shores, or even to a whole new world. Parents use leadership skills every single day as they take

> "One of the criticisms I've faced over the years is that I'm not aggressive enough or assertive enough, or maybe somehow, because I'm empathetic, it means I'm weak. I totally rebel against that. I refuse to believe that you cannot be both compassionate and strong."
>
> —FORMER NEW ZEALAND
> PRIME MINISTER
> JACINDA ARDERN

care of their family's life, managing healthcare, sports, transportation, schooling, general emotional well-being, making meals, schedules—you name it, parents do it.

Leaders are those who can inspire people to trust and follow them. They tend to burn brightly and boldly—but even a sizzling coal can start a forest fire.

* * ★ **CIVIC SUCCESS STORY** ★ * *

"I joined my county Democratic Party and was basically immediately ushered into canvassing for City Council and School Board candidates. I became a precinct leader and knocked on hundreds of doors for a City Council candidate who I believed had our city's best intentions in mind. She won! And, my precinct had a 3 percent higher turnout than the last odd election year. It made me feel amazing that, at the very least, I got people to exercise their right to vote."
—Kristen, age 34, Shawnee, Kansas

Characteristics

★ ★ ★

Forget tall, white, and handsome, we have a new set of characteristics we think applies to people who make the best civic leaders:

Confident: Whether it's your ideas, your values, your charisma, or just that you believe you are (morally, factually, ethically . . .) right, you are confident. People are drawn in by this confidence, and your tendency to speak up for your beliefs naturally ignites a passion in others to do the same.

Emotionally intelligent: You can walk into any room and read the crowd, from a dinner party to a work meeting, whether one person or 20. You see people for who they are, can figure out how to connect with them, and will probably have them joining your latest cause by the end of the day.

Bold: Look, sometimes this means that you are described as "difficult," but that's a badge we wear with pride. If you believe in something, you will proudly talk about it, and you know that the worst that can happen is someone says "no."

Galvanized: Your heart sings when you think of what's most meaningful to you. You hold an internal fire of intrinsic motivation. Sometimes this blends your own ambitions with achievements on behalf of causes you believe in, but your *why* is critical to your path.

Persuasive: You have that gift of convincing someone to go out to a party when they want to stay in. You use your emotional intelligence to read people and are confident and bold enough to push them toward your perspective. This doesn't mean you're bossy or overbearing, but that you find it easy to convince people to go along with you.

Types of Leaders

* ⭐ *

Within the civic space, we tend to see Leaders in three roles: leading movements, political campaigns, and policy change. Look through the following characteristics to see if any of them resonate with you and take that into consideration when thinking about how you can get civically engaged.

LEADING MOVEMENTS

Big political changes require crusaders at the forefront who push the boundaries of conversations, force issues to remain in the spotlight, help people's values evolve, and see a different vision for their community.

Rebellious: You are a Rebel With a Cause. To lead a movement, you can't be afraid to buck the status quo, question hegemony and the morass of cultural norms, while convincing others that something should and *can* change.

Insightful: There are people who have the gift of gab, but it's all about them. To be a true Leader is to be able to listen. To communicate with people in a way that sparks ideas and feelings in their soul. This takes a willingness and ability to really sit and hold emotional space for people, and then take action after deeper reflection.

LEADING POLITICAL CAMPAIGNS

Someone needs to keep the political trains running on time. Whether running for office or being a campaign manager, these people are our institutional powerhouses.

Competitive: Winning motivates you—or maybe on the flip side, losing makes you just a bit irrationally angry. You are the type of person who loves a proverbial horse race, and maybe you've dabbled in CrossFit, bullet journaling, or high school sports.

Undaunted: You're willing to take on a challenge, even when it's scary or you doubt you'll be able to succeed. You're the type of person who believes climbing mountains is possible if you put your mind to it. You're also willing to agitate and be unrelenting when you know someone will try to shut you down.

LEADING POLICY CHANGE

There's gotta be a head nerd in charge of coming up with new ideas.

Focused: If you want to get something done, you simply get it done. You don't pretend to be an expert in something, you become one. You are willing to put in the time and energy to really study something and become thoroughly informed about it.

Analytical: You have a gift for absorbing information and synthesizing it into something meaningful and practical beyond data output. Maybe you're into spreadsheets, mystery podcasts, or Taylor Swift's Easter eggs. Whatever your fixation, you always think on a second (and sometimes third) level.

* * ★ CIVIC SUCCESS STORY ★ * *

"I was part of the advocacy team that successfully expanded foster care in Louisiana, a hard-earned bipartisan legislative win for kids' services in a state that rarely strings those words together."
—Joy, age 43, New Orleans, Louisiana

LEADER:
Millicent Rogers, 38, Durham, NC

* * *

When Millicent Rogers's son was in kindergarten, she walked into his classroom one day and looked at the other volunteers. "He wasn't getting what he needed. He didn't see people that look like us volunteering in the schools." And so, Millicent stepped up to the plate for the first of what would be many times. For her, the decision to get involved was about one thing: her son. "If this means that my son's gonna get better outcomes, then I'm gonna have to be a helicopter mom. I'm gonna be there all day, every day, until they listen to me. I'm gonna show up. I'm gonna do the bulletin board. I'm gonna do all the things that the teacher asked for, if I can do those things. And if I can't do those things, I'm gonna find somebody else who can."

When you meet Millicent, she exudes a can-do confidence, and you know if she says she's going to do something . . . it will get done. But according to her, being a leader in her community wasn't the plan. Millicent went to college to be a teacher, then returned home to Durham, North Carolina, to be close to family and build a career in book sales and publishing.

As a first step, Millicent joined the PTA at her son's school. Then she moved into PTA leadership, and from there, when she saw the disparate funding of schools, she moved into state-level PTA leadership.

During these experiences she was gaining a deep under-standing of how the system works and what needed to be done to change it. At one point, the Teachers' Union wanted to bring a Community Schools partnership model into her son's school, which is where parents, educators, and school administrators take on the task of educating the whole child, reducing absenteeism, getting kids healthcare access, glasses, making sure they don't go hungry, and more. When the administration objected, Millicent started organizing, learning more about the intricacies of education policy, about who's who, and who's blocking key changes.

Eventually, she realized she wanted to push for changes to the PTA model, so she joined an advocacy organization called the People's Alliance. "I was a PTA mom just paying attention and realized the state needed to fund our schools. And we needed someone to speak up. We are 80 percent Black and brown students and we have mostly white parents going and advocating on the state level for the needs of . . . their students." She worked to change the meeting times and parent-teacher conferences so that working parents could attend without sacrificing a shift.

And then a door opened up when someone left the Durham Board of Education, and Millicent threw her hat into the ring for the appointment. She didn't get the job, and her takeaway was, "That meant there was more work to be done." She kept working and became president of the People's Alliance, pushing for accountability of state education officials. And she planned to stay in that role. "I live in an apartment. I don't have a washing machine and a dryer. I'm just one little person. And I decided that I was happy with the work that I was doing, advocating. And therefore I was not going to run for school board." But then she saw the people in power making the wrong choices, and she couldn't let that stand.

Millicent worked with the organization Run for Something,

which trains people to run for offices like school board, and ran. And she won. And if you ask her where she's headed next, she won't rule out statewide office.

Millicent's leadership is about calling others to service. When she was PTA president, a hurricane came through her community, and she organized a school cleanup. After talking to some of the parents who couldn't join, she realized there were members of her community without food. And so she organized delivery of food to the parents who needed it.

Her leadership is a combination of inviting people to the table and valuing them when they are there. "What I've learned is that people will do what you ask them to do, but they really want to be invited.... They want to feel special.... I just need five minutes of your time. Can you pick up trash for five minutes while you're in car-pool line? Or can you hand out these flyers? Can you make these copies for me? So just asking for a little bit of help from other people." It's very clear why people show up when Millicent asks; it's because she puts in the effort to see and value them. "When I'm advocating with people, I have to stop and ask them, *how are you doing?* It's not easy to advocate for yourself. It's not easy to advocate for your kids. It's not easy, especially when you are already part of a marginalized community. *How are you doing? Let's check in about you.* And sometimes people don't have anybody to ask them that. And once you ask them that, you invite them to the table to show up next time to do just a little bit."

Now that Millicent sits in a position of power, and not as an outside agitator, she has limitations. She has a fiduciary obligation that sometimes conflicts with what she would push for from the outside.

When asked how she thought she could do all this, Millicent says, "I didn't think I could do it. I knew that if I was gonna do it, I had to get a good team. And so I recruited other parents to come and join the work and figure out what we wanted it to be together . . . it's like how my family has always done it. You don't do everything. You do what you can, and you find people to surround yourself with who have a skill set that will enhance the work that you want to get executed."

Actions

★ ★ ★

A few hours a month:

▷ Attend school board meetings or town council meetings regularly and speak out when there's an issue you care about.

▷ Organize a group of your friends to be a political action pod— write letters together over brunch.

▷ Host a monthly club where you talk about current events (for instance: everyone reads articles about a certain news event, or you circulate a magazine article to discuss).

▷ Post on your socials about policy issues you care about.

▷ Volunteer to door knock or make calls for a local candidate.

▷ Sign up for the email list of an advocacy organization and follow their calls to action.

▸ Regularly attend the meetings of a social change group that works on an issue you care about (and when they ask for help at an event every once in a while, do so.)

A few hours a week:

▸ Join the legislative action committee of an advocacy group that's working on a policy issue you care about.

▸ Volunteer to be a precinct captain during elections. (These are people who serve as a connection between a political party and the voters in a precinct.)

▸ If there is a policy issue you have personal experience with, connect with an organization and volunteer to give testimony at a hearing.

▸ Run for or seek appointment to a local position like the zoning board or library board.

▸ Volunteer to help on a political campaign, for example help hand out yard signs.

▸ Write op-eds about policy issues in your local community for smaller news outlets and post on Facebook.

A full-time job:

▸ Run for office, work on campaigns or for elected officials.

▸ Find a position at an advocacy organization.

▸ Work as a clerk or policy analyst for the government.

▸ Work at a think tank or in academia on public policy.

Don't Let Imposter Phenomenon Get You Down

* ☆ *

Do you ever feel like the people who would make the best leaders are the ones who are least inclined to put themselves forward, and the least likely to hunger for the power and influence that come with leadership? Somewhere between feeling like an imposter and having an overinflated sense of self is the healthy self-esteem zone, and learning to separate a healthy level of self-esteem from a prolific ego is critical for a Leader who wants to guard against becoming an actual imposter.

The term "imposter syndrome," now known as imposter phenomenon,* was coined in 1978 by psychologists Pauline Rose Clance and Suzanne Imes to describe a phenomenon where high-achieving individuals are unable to internalize their accomplishments and fear being exposed as a fraud. Their study subjects were a group of high-achieving women from various professional fields who, despite their objective successes, felt they did not deserve their achievements and were constantly in fear of being exposed as undeserving. They tended to focus on evidence that supported their belief that they were imposters, while ignoring or downplaying evidence that contradicted it.

Although Clance and Imes's original study focused on women, subsequent research has shown that it can affect men and women alike. Further studies suggest that an estimated 70 percent of people

---

* While early research called it imposter syndrome, as it was thought to be somehow pathological, it's now referred to as the "imposter phenomenon" in research.

experience imposter phenomenon at some point in their lives,[2] and this prevalence cuts across different demographics, including age, gender, ethnicity, and profession.

Imposter phenomenon has consequences that reach far beyond the individual, and nowhere is this more evident than in the arena of political power and participation. The imposter phenomenon is a major impediment to diversity in political spaces, and thus in resulting policy. The adversarial and esoteric nature of discourse, the high financial and emotional costs, the complexity and bureaucracy, and the good old boys club (though the glass ceiling has more cracks) can all intensify feelings of being an imposter.

You may feel that you lack the expertise, the eloquence, or the credibility to engage in political dialogue, even on matters that directly affect you. This is by design, to ensure that America's halls of power maintain the spirit of a Norman Rockwell scene. The systems that were conceived by the most historically powerful individuals* were carefully designed to be inaccessible to those who don't fit their values and their aesthetic. They're incentivized to keep others out to maintain their own power, if not by law, then by norms. If not by norms, then by vibes. The imposter phenomenon is not necessarily your personal failing, but a legitimate feeling that reflects the intended outcome of institutions that were created to exclude you.

Engaging in civic life or activism inevitably requires speaking out and challenging prevailing norms and power structures. The experience of taking on such a role can be daunting. In practice, this results

---

* White, straight, wealthy, Christian men (statistically).

in women and people from marginalized communities, especially communities of color, being less likely to run for elected office. They know they'll be working twice as hard for half as much, with double the criticism. Lack of surety manifests as a reluctance to participate, not just in running for office but also in voicing one's opinions, joining campaigns, or leading grassroots or local movements.

We've heard countless times that people feel they aren't knowledgeable enough to be civically engaged, that they don't have a place at the table, and that getting a seat is about as realistic as getting through a Ticketmaster presale. To that we say: When has sounding like a completely ignorant moron ever stopped our elected officials? Never, that's when.

You're going to make mistakes, and even if you don't, we promise you will still feel stupid at one point or another. It'll pass, and no one was paying that much attention anyway. Move forward with a sprinkle of the delusion that your least favorite politician would proudly display.

Givers / EARTH

Summary

* ★ *

Givers are grounded doers whose actions are foundational to civic life. They are the backbone of any group, and the ones who can be counted upon to notice people's needs and do whatever they can to fulfill them. Deeply practical and action-oriented at heart, a Giver's bias toward generosity and compassion creates a sense of security for those around them, based in the knowledge that someone would have their back in a crisis.

"Don't tell me where your priorities are. Show me where you spend your money and I'll tell you what they are."

—JAMES W. FRICK

"My friend works for a property management company in D.C. She wrote a proposal to her company asking for a monetary donation to go towards supplies to hand out at the 2020 BLM march in D.C. She got the donation, and we worked together to package care kits for marchers—hand sanitizer, water, masks, snacks, etc. It was so powerful participating in that march and supporting the people protesting. My friend is such a badass for writing this proposal and finding money for this. She saw a need and got creative to find a solution."

—Lauren, age 37, Montgomery Village, Maryland

Characteristics

* ★ *

Altruistic: You most likely have an innate sense that you find comfort in giving to others. You may even feel that giving to others is one way you give to yourself, and not just because other people think highly of you, but because you genuinely derive contentment from it. This also makes other people more willing to accept from you, because they don't feel judgment or pride attached to it.

Generous: You're willing to split the last cookie in the pack, help carry the grocery bags, and share credit for a group project. You feel that a community's success is your success.

Project-loving: There are some people who just love a *project*. Whether it's the feeling of satisfaction from checking off that to-do list or being able to take on things where you can easily see the beginning, middle, and end, this is a personality trait whether the dictionary says it is or not.

Reliable: You're the one who holds a team project together and can be relied on to help when a friend has surgery. You believe that when you give someone your word, it's an agreement that can be counted on. Your trustworthiness is something that your friends know and value you for.

Nonjudgmental: Your philosophy is essentially live and let live. You meet people where they are and try to love them for that. You may get frustrated or disagree, but you don't judge or grudge.

FOR FACTS' SAKE:

Empathy vs. altruism: Empathy is how you feel toward others; it's the ability to extend beyond sympathy and understand another person's lived experience from within their frame of reference. It's the ability to put yourself in someone else's shoes. Altruism is the practice of helping others, and it can be for many different reasons—empathy, loyalty, philosophy, ideology, etc.

Types of Givers

⋆ ⋆ ⋆

Within the civic space, we tend to see Givers in three roles: giving time, giving money, and giving expertise. Look through the following characteristics to see if any of them resonate with you and take that into consideration when thinking about how you can get civically engaged.

GIVING TIME

The quintessential giver is someone who is always willing to show up, to drive a friend to a doctor's appointment, to volunteer at the animal shelter, to pray with someone when they need it. These are the moments that bind communities together; it's stopping to help someone with a flat tire or the proverbial helping an old lady cross the street.

Accepting: There's a difference between being tolerant and being open-minded. You naturally feel the humanity and worth of every person *simply because they're a person*, rather than because they're the type of person who one (or one's community) prefers, or because they've "earned" esteem and support.

Nonconformist: You're not the type to seek trouble, but you're probably not winning America's Next Top Rule Follower either. You aren't a fan of fitting in or fitting out (as part of the in-crowd or the out-crowd); you were the type in high school who had friends in all the cliques, and you aren't interested in being contrarian just for the hell of it. You would probably rather not be seen as contrarian, because being well liked and easily understood is a comfort that you are accustomed to and thrive on.

GIVING MONEY

If you care about maximizing efficiency in today's capitalistic world, there's a unit of measure we can use that allows you to transform your skills into the help people need most: cash. No shame in the efficiency game.

Practical: When someone calls you competent you take it as the highest compliment, you are pragmatic and reasonable, and you'll never hesitate to be scrappy or seek a unique, nonobvious solution. You're adept at making the most of what you have, even when resources are limited. You are a great compromiser and problem solver, especially in situations where idealism and/or extremism often hinder actual progress.

Efficient: If the real world could somehow function with the clarity of a controlled analysis, ah, peace would wash over you. You have an instinctive aversion to waste and suboptimal situations. You aren't precious or sentimental, you want to see people helped in the best and most efficient way possible.

GIVING EXPERTISE

You have specific and unique skills—you might use them to help a company earn coin or help your family stay on track. How can you pivot to helping your community with these same superpowers?

Conscientious: You appreciate structure and stability. You relish being an expert in your area of interest and take a great deal of pride in the thoroughness and solidity of your work. Hard boundaries and observable reality are your comforts in this unpredictable world (while many of us prefer snacks and scrolling on our phones).

Prudent: You care not only about the future, but about doing things correctly and knowing your limits. If you do something, you want to do it correctly and the best way you can.

"A few years ago, the Arlington County government proposed a large budget cut that would have taken away a shared resource for the local community theaters. Sitting on the board of one at the time, we got engaged—stuffed the ArlCo board meeting with people and testimony, wrote letters. While some changes were made, we successfully kept the resource open and available! (Because art matters!)"

—Lindsey, 41, Alexandria, Virginia

GIVER:
Jessica Rivera-Lucas, 43, Richardson, TX

★ ★ ★

Jessica is an educator and mom of three daughters who grew up in Brownsville, Texas, on the border with Mexico. Twelve years ago she moved with her family to the Dallas area and started volunteering. She mentors a civic engagement club at the local high school through an organization called March to the Polls; works with Hey Chica! to build excitement about voting in the Latine community; serves as the communications director for her local chapter of the League of Women Voters; and volunteered to help undocumented unaccompanied minors when they were separated from their parents. Even though today she is a super-volunteer, for Jessica, this has grown organically from when she first started. "I know it can be really scary—but it doesn't need to be hours of your day; sometimes it's just thirty minutes to call some people or an hour to hand out some information. It's funny the way volunteerism works—you start with an hour, but you are surrounded by so many wonderful people that you want to stay for more hours!"

She's inspired to do this work for four reasons: First, it is her mother who immigrated to this country from Mexico and who taught her to take the responsibility of citizenship seriously. Second, because of her faith, she believes that if you have the privilege to help someone, you should. The third reason is her daughters—she wants to set an example for her children that giving back is part of living in a community. And fourth is because, when she needed help, the community showed up to help her.

When Jessica talks about her work mentoring students, you can feel the palpable excitement in her voice. She loves working at the high school and says she really spends most of her time sitting in the corner and just helps them with planning or promotion of their ideas. This year, the club is hosting events to talk about immigration reform and brainstorming ways to raise community resources in addition to their voter registration work. "They come up with the most brilliant ideas of how to engage . . . they're so passionate and motivated. And I think that counters to what a lot of people have this perception of the younger generations. I love working with them."

When the government put out a call for volunteers because 1,500 unaccompanied children were being held in a detention facility, Jessica stepped up. As someone who speaks Spanish and has education experience, she felt called to volunteer and help. It was a "very emotional experience" for her, but she was able to play games, teach English, and help children who were otherwise receiving very little love and care.

Her volunteerism is about serving others, but that doesn't mean it hasn't enriched her own life: "Because of civic engagements I've built friendships I know I'll take with me till the last breath." For her, it's friendships built on shared values, other people who care about Black and brown people's access to voting, and the necessity to advocate to change that. "I talk to these people on the daily. They are my go-to people now outside of civic engagements. Sometimes when we just want to talk and vent about how expensive gas is! It definitely has built relationships that I hold near and dear to my heart."

Actions

★ ★ ★

A few hours a month:

▸ Make friends with your neighbors; let them know you're available when they need something. A cup of sugar, a ride somewhere, a babysitter, or just a call to say hi.

▸ Choose one or two organizations that are personally meaningful to you and make an annual donation or commitment to volunteer.

▸ Set up a mini-free-book library in your neighborhood and stock it.

▸ If you own a business, donate your products or services to charity auctions for causes you care about.

▸ Cultivate a mentality of generosity: when someone comes to you with a problem, approach the solution through a giving lens.

A few hours a week:

▷ Carve out a category of your personal budget for charitable contributions. Take some time to consider and research where you'd like to allocate funds, as well as a portion for reactive donations and new issues or needs that arise. Help your friends do the same.

▷ Volunteer regularly at a local service provider such as a shelter, soup kitchen, or community center.

▷ Collect secondhand donations within your neighborhood or workplace to distribute.

▷ Participate in your religious community's service mission in *your* neighborhood.

▷ Host a fundraiser on social media or IRL for a particular community need when it arises.

▷ Join the board of directors of a local organization or volunteer based on your expertise (for example, if you are an accountant— help organize the books.)

A full-time job:

▷ Pursue a career as a first responder, nurse, doctor, home health aide, social worker, or at an organization with a pro-social purpose.

▷ Become a major donor to an organization and sit on their board of directors, or work for a nonprofit as a full-time job.

▷ Develop a pro bono practice or an in-kind donation system at your workplace.

Fighting Selfishness with Generosity and Self-Interest with Community Care

* * *

Citizens United probably isn't joining *Roe v. Wade* in the graveyard anytime soon, which means that a Giver is more critical in this environment than ever. The issue of money's influence on elected officials, and the resulting policies they help enact or repeal, is not a simple one, but the only attempts at solutions don't need to come from within the legislative or court systems. If anything, waiting for the legislative or court systems to do something is like waiting for rain in a drought: it's disappointing.

The most obvious way of thinking about solutions is to fight money with other money, and match spending on the policies that you don't like with spending on policies you do. This is essentially what's already happening and part of the reason why the GDP of the political economy (campaign costs, vendors, consultants, advertising) grows with every cycle. It's also a solution that's available to only a few hundred or thousand very wealthy individuals, though there's nothing that's stopping anyone who has a Giver soul but not a big budget from managing their personal donations and spending in a purposeful and ethical way that aligns with their values. The same goes if your professional, charitable, or extracurricular role gives you authority to do so.

Stepping into your Giver identity is about your approach to distribution of resources more than it's about the quantity you're distributing. If anyone's ever asked you to be treasurer of a club because you're the only one who can be trusted, you probably exude a Giver's best qualities without even trying. Especially within community or nonprofit organizations, individuals can use the power of the purse to steer the future of those organizations, and results can range from disastrous to life-changing.

Success is often determined by sheer resources, which are limited in more cases than not, meaning that it usually comes down to allocating for the greatest impact, without waste and (it should go without saying) fraud. Whether it's figuring out how to fund a local renovation, helping a nonprofit distribute aid, or managing the baked goods budget of your mahjong club, a Giver has both the sense and trustworthiness to make sure every dollar is used optimally. And they'll never miss an opportunity to press that cash-back button.

Givers are like advertisements: you can find them almost anywhere. They're frequently employed through the political system directly or extra-governmentally, such as through financial or nonprofit investments in underserved communities. It also doesn't have to be purely about dollars. You can also help build more equitable institutions and workplace structures. For example, if you're in a position to hire people or to award certain opportunities, those decisions are opportunities for ethical distribution. Even if you have no say in anything, but your manager or colleague or anyone else you know does, there can be opportunities to advocate for a particular person, compensation, or budget structure. Someday *you* might be the boss, so best to start practicing now.

Connectors / WATER

Summary

★ ★ ★

Connectors are empaths who can seep into even the most disconnected parts of their communities. As the living embodiments of "the more the merrier," Connectors are inclusive by nature and eager to bring people together at any opportunity. Walking down the street with a Connector feels like you're with Belle in *Beauty and the Beast* as she merrily greets the townspeople. In an era of intense loneliness and isolation, we especially need to recognize the friendly faces who weave the fabric of communities with their social skills; easy to dismiss but truly the life force that keeps us going.

"People wanted this imaginary character to fix their problems. . . . I want to use my platform to remind people that they're the fixers in their communities. They're the change-makers and the problem-solvers in their lives, in their families, in their neighborhoods, in their school boards, and in their states."

—KERRY WASHINGTON

Characteristics

★ ★ ★

Empathetic: You may consider yourself an empath or a highly sensitive person. Your feelings are always floating on the surface, and you easily feel the pain and joy of those around you. You are authentic and easy in a way that leads others to feel seen and connected.

Gracious: You exude a natural sociability and have an easy time speaking to many different types of people, including those who are very different from you. This doesn't mean you're necessarily gregarious, but it's a comfort being with other people.

Spontaneous: You love to find novelty and avoid environments that demand uniformity or discourage individual expression. You enjoy being able to express your curiosity and social savvy whenever the whim hits you. Your joie de vivre is appreciated by all who seek to be around you.

Intuitive: You have an ability to see how groups fit together and have a strong sense of interpersonal dynamics. Your emotional intelligence allows you to walk into a room and see how you can bring people together, or in favor of your most recent cause. Your capacity for vulnerability resonates with people, so they typically connect to you quickly on a more intimate level.

Patient: Like Rome, a community isn't built in a day. Whether it's patience with people or working through the growing pains that inevitably come with even the most positive changes, you're willing to put in the extra effort to work through something. Or on the flip side, you're willing to be patient for others to reach their own conclusions.

Types of Connectors

★　★　★

Within the civic space, we tend to see Connectors in three roles: connecting politics and people, connecting the hearts of a community together, and connecting helpers with the people who need help. Look through the following characteristics to see if any of them resonate with you and take that into consideration when thinking about how you can get civically engaged.

CONNECTING POLITICS AND PEOPLE TOGETHER

There is a vast chasm between the institutions that run our towns, cities, and country and the people who make up the democracy that (ostensibly) runs this country. We need people to connect the complicated morass of politics to the people (and vice versa).

Confident: You are a source of guidance and—dare we say—inspiration to people around you. You're probably a little less flashy than the people who get top billing on the political ticket, but you're often the first stop when someone needs a solution or assistance.

Knowledgeable: You know how the sausage gets made, who to talk to, or (at least) where to go to talk to the right people. It doesn't matter if your CV is full of practical experience or if you have learned through practice the "ways things work." You know what you need to know to get results.

CONNECTING THE HEARTS
OF A COMMUNITY TOGETHER

The spirit of a community is defined by its people. Whether that's coming together for a holiday dinner, a local sports team, a bake sale to help a senior home, or something a bit grander, moments of togetherness lead to experiences and feelings that bond us.

Inclusive: You love to hang out with people, and they love to hang out with you; you also love to introduce your friends to your other friends, plan a party or a meetup. You easily connect with people and make it easy to nurture relationships with many different types of people who have a range of perspectives and lived experiences.

Compassionate: You don't have to understand what someone is experiencing to feel for them. You are aware of what other people are going through, and you have a strong desire to alleviate it. You're often described as warm and kindhearted, even by people you've just met.

CONNECTING HELPERS WITH
THE PEOPLE WHO NEED HELP

Train stations need conductors, but they also need station agents. You might be one of the often overlooked people who form the backbone of the community, using your connective nature to help fulfill everyone's needs thoughtfully and efficiently.

Responsible: You take pride in your willingness to step up to challenges, are often the one to raise your hand to volunteer, and at minimum are the one who helps split the check. You don't do it for the credit, but because you enjoy the sense of satisfaction you get from delivering and helping people around you.

Introspective: You are often examining your own self and purpose in this life. You think about what you can offer, and sometimes question your role. Your time spent learning about yourself isn't for naught, it means that you are better equipped to see others who are also looking for help.

CONNECTOR:
Jen Perez, 42, Cincinnati, OH
★ ★ ★

Jen calls herself a data-coding nerd. She spent twenty years working at a Fortune 500 company, moving from intern all the way up to managing 250 engineers across the globe. But in 2022 she started feeling like something was off in her life; she was burnt out from having a young daughter at home, and the stress of the pandemic was weighing on her. She felt like she was living "the dream," but not *her* dream. And so she walked away from the only career she ever knew. It felt "much bigger than leaving a job."

Jen wasn't particularly political, but she has a personal history with reproductive healthcare. She had an incomplete miscarriage that required a D&C and intensive medical care that saved her life. When the Supreme Court decision came down overturning *Roe v. Wade* and a six-week abortion ban immediately went into place in Ohio, she started getting activated. She thought to herself—would I have survived with the six-week ban?

She was constantly texting and talking to her friends about politics, and when she found the organization Red Wine & Blue she realized she could do the same thing as part of a team. Red Wine & Blue does something called relational organizing, which really just means talking about politics with people you know and encouraging them to engage. "How do we empower women to have these conversations about issues that are important to me? Instead of just talking about how upsetting the *Dobbs* decision was with people who agreed with me, it encouraged me to start the conversation or broach it with people that maybe I was a little unsure of." The organization helped her feel empowered, giving her resources to talk about Ohio's pressing issues with people she met at the gym or at her kids' soccer games.

She realizes, looking back, that she was always connecting people with ideas and opportunities in her job. Convincing people to get on board with your ideas is how you survive in a huge corporation, but she had never thought of that as who she was until she started volunteering. She wasn't even that political; she voted but didn't keep track of all the small elections and nuances in her community.

In the summer of 2023, Ohio went through a referendum process to protect abortion access, and one of the first steps in that process was collecting signatures. When we think about collecting signatures, we often think of people standing on the street and accosting strangers, but the way Red Wine & Blue works is different—they ask you to go to your friends and neighbors, people you know, and talk about it. Because it was about more than just the signature, it was about building a coalition of people who would vote when the time comes. In that election there was so much disinformation flying around—mailers and a lot of noise; what Jen found was that, "if you have a relationship you're going to be able to cut through that noise."

After volunteering for a few months, Jen ended up taking a job as an organizer with Red Wine & Blue and started building out a huge network of people, talking to friends and family about the referendum. We so often think about it as just talking, but what Jen realized through her experiences is that conversations are how you build political power—"I just have this one conversation and open someone's eyes to a different perspective. And I'm not sure they would have been open to the conversation if it hadn't been me. And that's pretty cool, right? I mean, that's really empowering."

And the thing about all those conversations is, they added up to a big win, and Jen was a part of protecting reproductive healthcare in her state. Today she's talking about school boards and having conversations on the importance of protecting kids in schools, because she's seen, through personal experience, the political power of conversation.

Actions

★ ★ ★

A few hours a month:

▶ Help friends and family fill out their ballots during election season.

▶ Use your social media to gain insight into other people's perspectives by connecting with people outside your echo chamber.

▶ Host regular potluck dinner parties where you invite people from different walks of life to come together.

▶ Post who you are voting for on your socials and share election resources.

▶ Help people you know who are looking for jobs by making introductions, sharing their résumé, or giving helpful advice in an informational interview.

▶ Go to city/town events and bring your friends; look out for seasonal and holiday events.

A few hours a week:

▶ Start and manage a book club with monthly in-person meetings.

▶ Volunteer to door-knock, fundraise, or phone bank for your favorite candidate.

▶ Get educated on how things work in your community: How does political change happen? What are the systems? Learn who the players are, then develop relationships with the people in charge. Start with a town hall or school board meeting.

▶ Become a mentor for someone whose future you could change for the better.

▶ Donate a product or service to a local organization.

▶ Recruit your friends to run for office.

▶ Volunteer to organize civic events like holiday parties, girl scouts, or read-a-thons.

▶ Get more involved with local politics and focus on bringing people to events and meetings that you know will interest them.

▶ Learn the skill of deep canvassing (a.k.a. relational organizing) and build a network of connectors who share information.

A full-time job:

▶ Cultivate a career as a master networker—a recruiter/head-hunter, fundraiser, or matchmaker.

▶ Work as an event planner, organizing events that bring people together, or volunteer your planning skills.

▶ Get involved in mentorship or networking groups.

▶ Work as a full-time relational organizer for a nonprofit.

You've Got to Have Friends

* * *

In an age of loneliness and eroding democracy, friendship is both an act of resistance and a literal lifesaver.

In May 2023, the Office of the Surgeon General published an extensive report titled *Our Epidemic of Loneliness and Isolation*, an advisory on the health risks of loneliness and the healing effects of social connection and community. The report found that even before the Covid-19 pandemic, approximately half of U.S. adults reported experiencing measurable levels of loneliness.

Perhaps more headline-worthy was how devastating they concluded the physical consequences of loneliness can be. Researchers quantified the risk of premature death associated with lacking social connections as comparable to smoking 15 cigarettes a day. The report warned of a 29 percent increased risk of heart disease, 32 percent increased risk of stroke, and a 50 percent increased risk of developing dementia for older adults.[1]

Interestingly, it concluded that the negative effects of loneliness aren't about the number of people that someone has around them, but the quality and depth of their connections with those people. It also found that people ages 15–24 had 70 percent less in-person social interaction than that cohort did twenty years ago—digital media having replaced the social interactions that historically occupied much of our lives.

As terrible as the loneliness spiral can be for an individual, the harm to us as a collective is also incredibly serious.

Holocaust survivor, historian, and political philosopher Hannah Arendt wrote extensively about authoritarianism and extremism, and her work emphasized the centrality of friendship to her own political philosophy and survival, as well as the importance of social ties as a shield against the spread of fascism. She argued that "totalitarian movements are mass organizations of atomized isolated individuals . . . such loyalty [to the state] can be expected only from the completely isolated human being who, without any other social ties to family, friends, or even mere acquaintances, derives his sense of having a place in the world only from his belonging to a movement, his membership in the party."[2]

Isolation and loneliness can make individuals vulnerable to becoming supporters of extremist regimes, while the mere act of having friends and authentic connections does the opposite: it makes an aspiring autocratic regime more vulnerable.

Caring might lead to much more frustration and pain than apathy, but this is where the gifts of genuine relationships and strong social ties shine through. Anyone who's ever experienced grief or held on to a secret can attest that a shared burden is a lessened burden, and this is true when it comes to struggles in the political sphere. Today's loneliness is why we need Connectors, people who are pros at truly seeing those around them and making them feel like they are being seen, like they matter, like they're accounted for.

Creators / AIR

Summary

★ ★ ★

A Creator's work is the oxygen of democracy. Freedom of expression is a condition for creating art, and it's no coincidence that the arts are always a prime target in autocratic societies. The freedoms that underpin democracy (speech, religion, assembly, protest) are what allow Creators to use their varied talents to capture the shared emotions and experiences of individuals, communities, and the human condition. Like the wind, you don't have to see it, or even know its source, to recognize the power of artistry to move us. Creators come in many stripes, but their shared gift is the ability to capture intangible feelings and translate them into a beautiful language of mutual understanding, in the service of bringing people together.

> "What is freedom of expression? Without the freedom to offend, it ceases to exist."
>
> — SALMAN RUSHDIE

Characteristics

✶ ✶ ✶

Open-minded: You are the type of person who can create something out of nothing—or rather, merely from your own ideas and feelings. You are open to new ideas and experiences and are willing to see where life takes you.

Unconventional: You aren't the type to say, *We should do it this way because that's how it's always been done.* You see the potential beyond the status quo to explore new ideas and "what ifs." Your creativity is fueled by an intuitive gift for seeing possibilities that others don't. Beyond that, you often feel lukewarm about adhering to structure and have few qualms about shirking conventions.

Skeptical: You are not often willing to just accept any answer; you have doubts about what people say and if they are really revealing the truth. But on the other hand, one of your favorite maxims is *When people show you who they are, believe them.*

Curious: You're the type to always be reading and seeking out new information. You genuinely enjoy learning about new subjects, even if doing so provides no immediate material value to you.

Expressive: Albert Einstein once said that "if you can't explain it simply, you don't understand it well enough," and frankly, who would know better than he? You can meet people at their level of understanding because you love the energy that builds when people are excited about the same thing. You don't just tell people information, you communicate with feeling.

Restless: It's hard for you to sit still (literally or metaphorically). You are excited about the next thing to do, see, or think about, and you want to bring others along for the ride. Your restlessness is a superpower.

Types of Creators

* ★ *

Within the civic space, we tend to see Creators in three roles: creating messages, creating art, and educating others. Look through the following characteristics to see if any of them resonate with you and take that into consideration when thinking about how you can get civically engaged.

CREATING MESSAGES

While truth itself is something that just exists, the messages and information that make it understandable and digestible to the rest of us are something that needs to be created. For the wheels of democracy to turn, it's important to have people out there making sure people know what's up, spreading news, and fighting disinformation.

Objective: You believe that there's such a thing as verifiable reality, and that empirical truth is the foundation of that reality. You try to make judgments and draw conclusions that are based in reality, rather than in your feelings, to the fullest extent possible.

Analytical: You have a keen eye for spotting discrepancies and inconsistencies, and you're innately skeptical of conventional wisdom. You're always looking for evidence to challenge a questionable narrative and are unafraid to change your mind when presented with new information. You're fluent in discerning reliable sources, identifying inconsistencies, and calling out misleading information, even when sifting through massive amounts of data. You're committed to verifying the accuracy of information before you feel comfortable standing it up as fact.

CREATING ART

The creatives of the world are incredible at sharing stories and amplifying values and narratives that shape our civic life. These are the marketers, artists, and translators who amplify what we experience.

Technological: You are social media fluent, and beyond that, you're willing to learn the highways and byways of information to disseminate messages that matter. You care not only about using technology, but learning how it works and how to maximize it, though you're aware of its pitfalls as well.

Aesthete: You are artistic, imaginative—a creative in the traditional sense. You may have a vision for art, music, writing, performing, designing, architecting, cooking, taking part in any of the myriad Oscar categories required to produce visual media, or creating in any of the various media that we normally categorize as art. More important, you love and value using creativity to inspire, educate, and transform.

EDUCATING OTHERS

Making sure people understand what is happening is how we preserve a robust democracy. This isn't about just teaching kids, but also newcomers, neighbors, and friends.

Tactful: You're able to deliver messages, teach, and inform without making people feel judged. No matter how much support someone may objectively need, no one wants to feel like a charity case. You have a critical soft skill: the ability to help with grace in a way that preserves the receiver's dignity.

Inventive: You're always coming up with new ideas, and you're willing to consider almost anything.

CREATOR:
Erin Bauchan-Caprara, 35, Kalamazoo, MI

Erin, an insurance agent by day, was looking for a hobby a few years ago. Her grandfather, whom she was very close to, passed away, and then, shortly thereafter, her dog died. She couldn't find a therapist with space and needed an outlet for her emotions. She became interested in sewing with the goal of creating her own clothes, but got intimidated by the complicated constructions. So instead she decided to take up quilting.

At the same time, she had been thinking deeply about politics and gun violence in this country and was feeling very powerless. She started building a quilt memorializing all the incidents of mass gun violence in the United States in 2024 with tick marks (four lines and then a fifth going across).

At first this was a hobby and a solitary effort for Erin, but now she's built a community of quilters who have made quilts about gun violence, and they are working together to put on an exhibition. She's also joined a quilting group at a local store and has made friends in that space.

While many think of quilting as a crafts project, it's also an art form with a history of protest. For Erin, the juxtaposition of the coziness we associate with quilts and the jarring reality of gun violence in this country further emphasizes her political point.

Through her art she's been able to start conversations—with neighbors, with other artists, and with people on instagram as @seamrippersociety. Erin has turned a search for a therapist into a hobby and now into political action.

Actions

* ⭐ *

A few hours a month:

▸ Seek out and support artists who represent your values; share their work and attend their events.

▸ Raise civically engaged children; bring them to vote, to protest, and encourage them to write a letter to their representatives. (They will often respond!)

▸ Make sure people around you know they can ask you their "stupid" questions about politics.

▸ Create and maintain a free guide or information resource for your community, such as a list of local recommendations to share with new neighbors, a recipe recommendation bank, or an annual voter guide.

A few hours a week:

▶ Volunteer to help manage social media for a campaign or organization you care about.

▶ Create content about a cause you care about for your own channels.

▶ Organize events for kids that help them learn about the political process.

▶ Take a class to learn a new art form.

▶ Join local Facebook groups and combat misinformation when you see it (noting this can get heated).

▶ Develop an artistic hobby and join with others in your community to craft.

A full-time job:

▶ Pursue a career as a journalist, data scientist, researcher, teacher, or pundit.

▶ Start a political social media account or a column in your local newspaper.

▶ Volunteer at a local museum, performing arts center, or library.

▶ Create and share art with political resonance.

Art Is a Vessel for Values

★ ★ ★

Art reflects values, and artists and creators are often at the forefront of cultural progress. Through their work, a Creator can demonstrate society's potential, because art and entertainment can penetrate the public consciousness to present new or so-called radical ideas in a digestible way.

Take the evolution of norms around marriage equality. In the 1990s, the national conversation was primarily centered on allowing civil unions for same-sex couples at best. Full marriage equality was not even a bullet point on the mainstream agenda at that time (though it was most definitely on the agenda of people who wanted same-sex marriage), and not a single nationally elected official would claim it on their platform.

Almost twenty years after Ellen DeGeneres came out as a lesbian on her TV show (1997) and the sitcom *Will and Grace* premiered (1998), the landmark Supreme Court decision *Obergefell v. Hodges* affirmed the constitutional right to marriage equality in 2015. Entertainment has the power to introduce new possibilities, set new norms, and the potential to stir souls and change the opinions of large swaths of people at once. If it weren't such a threat, there wouldn't be such a widespread obsession with book banning within (aspiring) autocratic regimes.

So, keep imagining and creating. You never know whose life you may have already changed or will in the future.

STATEMENT SERENADERS:
A Musical History of Protest

★ ★ ★

"We Shall Overcome" (1901): A century-old gospel song rooted in African American folk traditions that became a prominent protest anthem during the Civil Rights Movement. Modern versions are lyrically descended from a hymn written by gospel singer Charles Albert Tindley, and it's been performed by dozens of artists over several decades.

"Strange Fruit," Billie Holiday (1939): "Strange fruit" is a euphemism to represent the lynching of Black Americans. It was originally written as a poem by the Jewish American writer Abel Meeropol. Holiday's record label resisted her recording the song in fear of backlash in the South (unheard of), but she fought to get it produced by another record label and then sold more than a million copies.

"Fortunate Son," Creedence Clearwater Revival (1969): A counterculture anthem about the Vietnam War draft, which the children of the wealthy were able to avoid.

"Ohio," Crosby, Stills, Nash & Young (1970): Another Vietnam-era banger, this song was written and rush-released after the band saw photos in *Life* magazine of four students at Kent State University who were killed by the Ohio National Guard while protesting the Vietnam War. It took another five years for the U.S. to fully exit Vietnam, and people played this song on repeat the whole time.

"Hurricane," Bob Dylan (1975): A seven-minute folk-rock song that Dylan wrote to narrate and publicize the story of Rubin "Hurricane" Carter, a Black champion boxer who was arrested for murder. The song accuses the police of racial profiling Carter and an unfair trial at which he was convicted. Ultimately, he was imprisoned until he was released following a petition of habeas corpus 20 years later.

"Zombie," The Cranberries (1994): An alternative rock/grunge song written in response to a terrorist bombing by the IRA that killed two children in Warrington, England. The band was reportedly offered $1 million by their record label to work on a "less politically charged" song, to which front woman Dolores O'Riordan responded by ripping up the check.[1]

"American Skin (41 Shots)," Bruce Springsteen (2001): Written in response to the 1999 police shooting of Amadou Diallo, this song led the New York City police union, the Patrolmen's Benevolent Association, to call for a boycott of Springsteen's shows. This is significant because if there's any constituency that's core to Bruce's fandom, it's tri-state-area cops.

"American Idiot," Green Day (2004): Although this was written during the Iraq War, the band has stated that it's not about the 43rd president, but was intended to call out the mass media for stirring up paranoia, fear, and xenophobia following 9/11. You would think they would've named it "American Idiots" (plural) to avoid such inevitable confusion, but we suspect they may have just said that because they were afraid of getting Dixie Chicks'ed.

"Born This Way," Lady Gaga (2011): An equality anthem that Gaga credited as inspired by the gay Black minister and AIDS activist Archbishop Carl Bean. He was a disco singer who wrote and sang "I Was Born This Way" a decade before Gaga was even born, and she publicly thanked him when she celebrated the song's ten-year anniversary in 2021.

"Black Parade," Beyoncé (2020): Released in celebration of Juneteenth in 2020, shortly after the murder of George Floyd. Upon winning the Grammy in 2021 for Best R&B Performance, Beyoncé became the most awarded singer and female artist in Grammy history.

SECTION 5:
AN ACTION PLAN TO GET STARTED

WHETHER YOU FLIPPED HERE directly or you've diligently read Sections 1–4, you might be thinking, *OKAY, SO WHAT DO I DO, THOUGH?!* Rather than tell you to start writing out a task list for changing the world (What would you put on there? Run for office? Call your congressperson? Scream into the abyss???), this section is full of steps to help you build an action plan with sustainable ways to integrate civic engagement into your life.

Audit Your
News Consumption

THE FIRST THING WE THINK you should do is audit your current sources of information. This seems simple but in fact is a critical part of your civic equation. Becoming informed isn't passive; it's a way to learn what's happening, who the players are, and how to get involved before things turn into a crisis. It shapes your reality, and is a resource for you to learn more about the issues that affect you and your family's life.

Our questions here are: How do you consume your news? Do you feel like it informs you, or does it just stir your emotions? What emotions does it stir? Is it biased, factual, enraging, coming at you live from the depths of an echo chamber? And of course—how can you develop a news diet that keeps you informed without driving you to disengagement?

Assess Your Current News Diet:

Write: All the ways you currently consume news, and *when* you consume it.

What: Social media? Cable news? A paperboy tossing the *New York Times* at the end of your driveway? A quartet of male podcasters?

Consider: What local/state/national news sources are you reading or watching? What method do you enjoy consuming most: audio, video, or print? (The one that holds your attention best is probably going to be the one you stay consistent with.)

When: Are you keeping up with news only in the morning? In bits and spurts throughout the day? Once a week? Once a month?

. . . And How Does That Make You Feel?

▸ Ask yourself if you feel you are getting the type of information about the subjects you want. Are they helping or hindering your understanding of what's going on?

▸ Does your news consumption tend to leave you feeling more informed or overwhelmed? Engaged or cynical? Do you feel that the news you consume merely acts to spark emotions, sharing the shallow basics of a story, or does it make you feel better informed?

▸ It's normal that hearing upsetting news will elicit an emotional response, but the question is whether your sources of choice are sending you to emotional highs so much that it makes you want to stop learning about the news at all. Your emotional response is a clue to which sources you might want to reconsider.

Design Your Intentional News Diet:

▸ Here's where you take control. Start by carefully selecting outlets you trust to be your *regular* news sources. Aim for a mix.

▸ Pick the voices you want to hear, based on the perspectives and issues you prioritize. (There is no right answer!) Maybe that means signing up for newsletters from independent journalists with trusted expertise in areas of personal interest. Perhaps it's a podcast to keep ready for car rides. The key is to choose sources that inform, engage, and align with your values, while not completely ensconcing yourself in an impenetrable echo chamber.

▸ Actively seek out and follow the social accounts of creators and news outlets, as algorithms often suppress this type of content.

▸ Eliminate sources that share unreliable information from your feed to the best of your ability. Freely block and/or report troll accounts and toxic personalities who are known for spreading disinformation. Change your settings to block certain words and topics from your feed. It's not possible to control everything, but at a minimum, you can be a conscious digital consumer.

▸ Sign up for local news updates and subscribe to a local paper. Both will be extremely helpful for getting involved in your closest community, as this is where you'll find most official announcements and information about what's going on.

▸ Consider the impacts of your news consumption and set boundaries. If the headlines are feeding your anxiety, set a specific time to read or listen to prevent unproductive doomscrolling.

▸ Don't confuse your misery over politics with doing something about it, and don't let your misery drain your energy so you're too depleted to do anything. If political gridlock promises anything, it's that you're not missing any problems that won't still be here tomorrow.

When you finish this exercise, go to page 181,
"Bringing It All Together," and write down a few notes.

CIVIC SUCCESS STORIES:
SHARING ON SOCIAL MEDIA

"Friends have shared that some of what I post makes them do their own research. Which is honestly my goal. I don't want people just blindly following me or anyone else."

—Becca, age 41, Shawnee, Kansas

"I generally don't engage with trolls or go looking for the cesspool comment sections. I don't watch mainstream media. As Mr. Rogers says, I look for the helpers. Where are the people sharing good info and doing good things. I curate my feed to largely be people active in political advocacy and sharing my same passions. Not to create an echo chamber but because I've found it is excellent peer pressure to educate me and encourage me to be braver in what I say and post—both online and in real life."

—Kaleena, age 35, Madison, Wisconsin

"When current political events upset me, I share them on my Instagram. I post information about that current situation, paired with my commentary that either expands the explanation, provides context, or my opinions about it. I guess it both allows me to vent, engage with people about it if they reply to my story, and at the very least I know I'm keeping other people informed. When I can't do anything else about a frustrating situation, at least I can keep others informed."

—Anna, age 34, Chicago, Illinois

"I don't post on social media a lot, but when I do it's usually about an action that I want other people to join. I'm proud to have encouraged others to donate or join me for a phone bank/text bank/postcard event."

—Amy, 68, Davis, California

Create Your Civic Calendar

IN THE AGE OF INFORMATION OVERLOAD, staying up-to-date on local events remains a daunting task, even for the most intensely engaged. And we should clarify that consuming information about politics and actually engaging in civic life are two different things. For step two, we are asking you to set up a calendar of the civic events and elections you care most about to get into the practice of showing up for your community.

There's no single place that we can direct everyone to find all this information, and there is no single civic calendar that works for everyone. What's important is for you to create your *personal* calendar, one that reflects your interests, values, and physical location. (And as always, this can change!)

IN GENERAL

Follow and Sign Up: If an organization or lawmaker you care about has a mailing list, social media account, or other way to stay informed about meetings and decisions, sign up.

Save the Dates: Put any relevant meetings or events on your calendar, even if you aren't sure if you want to go.

Show Up: Whether it's on Zoom or IRL, showing up to something is an action in and of itself. It's a way to get informed, build community, and start learning more about the topics you care about. Look, we know how hard it is to resist the urge to cancel plans for things we *like* to do, but the hardest part is usually just getting out the door. Plus, this is how you build friendships and connections!

TRACK UPCOMING ELECTIONS

Research Your Elected Officials: Make a list of all the elected officials who represent you, and investigate them like you suspect they're a serial killer who just started dating your best friend.

Identify Upcoming Elections: Check for local, state, and national dates. They're not always on the same Tuesday in November.

Research Candidates: Know who's running and their platforms. Ballotpedia is a helpful source to start.

Write It Down: Put these dates on your calendar. Don't forget to take into consideration registration deadlines, early voting, and absentee voting guidelines. Make sure you're registered!

IDENTIFY LOCAL GOVERNING BODIES

Identify the Local Political Bodies That You Care About: School board? Library board? Town council? Pick one or more you'd like to focus on.

Find Information Sources: Where do they share information about meetings and topics? The town's website? Facebook? Bulletin boards? Carrier pigeon? Figure this out once and you'll be set forever.

POLITICAL ADVOCACY GROUPS

Identify Your Priorities: What activates you? Gun reform? Education? Healthcare? (Check back in with your mission statement from Section 3.) Start with one that you want to focus on and scale up from there.

Find Advocacy Groups: Is there a national group with a state or local chapter that aligns with your views? Go on their website to look it up. Aren't sure where to start? Ask some friends, check out social media channels, and google around. Want to find something super local? Investigate who is quoted in the local newspaper or posting in the local Facebook group to get more information and a better sense of whether the group is going to be your vibe. You can always start at one group and move to another until you find the right fit.

Find Political Action Groups / Government Affairs Committee: Are you a member of a group that is already organizing politically? For example, a professional or religious organization? These groups might already have advocacy committees, or there might be national organizations that do. Most unions and professional groups have a governmental affairs group. Sometimes large companies have pro bono advocacy committees. (The moral complexities of which are a book in and of themselves, but they are a good way to gain knowledge from experts in the field.)

POLITICAL PARTIES (IF DESIRED)

Pick Your Party: Your political party likely has local, state, and national groups you can join. If you care about lots of different issues or just want to dip your toes into campaigns, this is a great place to start.

Volunteer: You might find that most of your local political groups are filled with boomers who likely will want your help doing things like posting on TikTok. There are lots of volunteer opportunities, from door knocking to cold calling, but helping build the infrastructure of your local civic community is an often overlooked option.

IT DOESN'T HAVE TO BE POLITICAL AT ALL

Nonprofits: Giving back to your community is an innately political action. If you're looking for something more fundamentally charitable but completely nonpartisan, volunteers are consistently needed in numerous capacities. Things like organizing food and clothing drives or donating your time to a shelter are always going to make a difference to people's immediate needs.

Community Building: Time spent bonding with friends, going out of your way to spend an extra ten minutes getting to know your neighbors, and just making casual conversation with those who surround us all are small blocks that increase social cohesion and strengthen humanity's connections to each other. And since we're the founders of this framework, we'd rule it constitutional that merely getting your head out of your phone and making eye contact with another human is an act of positive civic engagement.

> When you finish this exercise, go to page 182,
> "Bringing It All Together," and write down a few notes.

★ ★ ★ **CIVIC SUCCESS STORY** ★ ★ ★

"In 2020, Colorado repealed the death penalty. The previous fall, a friend and I went to a meeting with the local ACLU to write postcards and letters to the editor. I had my letter published in a small local paper and also wrote to my State House rep about it. The ACLU was a big part of getting the death penalty repealed in a debate that was contentious because of the Aurora Theater Shooting, but I was thrilled when the effort succeeded."

—Kasey, 37, Golden, Colorado

Build a Civic Network Without "Networking"

THE POWER OF CIVIC ENGAGEMENT to fight loneliness and add meaning to our lives is rooted in the personal connections we build. But to do that you have to make friends. For most of us, it's super daunting to show up at a new place without knowing anyone, but the reward is sweet. There's something incredibly special about the relationships you have with people who share your values (not just your interests), the people who also want to spend a Tuesday night learning the intricacies of education policy or talk about what's happening in a commerce committee. And inevitably, as you face hardship and success, everything is richer and sweeter when experienced with friends.

✦ ✶ ★ CIVIC SUCCESS STORY ★ ✶ ✦

"I got one of my good friends to register to vote for the very first time in his life a couple of years ago! He's in his late 40s, and now we have a tradition of sitting down to fill out our ballots together!"
—Kimberly, 44, Oakland, California

Reflect:

▸ Look back to your three personal mission statements in Section 3. How are you manifesting those in your everyday life? Are there elements of your current lifestyle, environment, or peers that conflict with those values?

Set Some Goals:

▸ If you're looking to get out into your community more, what are the things you're seeking and/or open to? New friendships? A passion project? Just in the mood to give back without any specific purpose? Consider if you have time to add new commitments to your plate, or if the goal is to figure out how to reframe your current activities to better align with your values.

Find Your People:

▸ Going to events, joining advocacy groups or communities of faith, and volunteering on campaigns are some of the obvious ways to get civically active. There are many opportunities both in real life and online to build community around issues you care about, and super-local projects (helping clean up a playground, debating a new speed bump, etc.) are often an easy first step and a great way to meet neighbors.

▸ Reach out to people who are already involved in those initiatives to see if they'd be willing to help you learn more about what the commitment is, what the vibe is, and maybe even to attend your first meeting or event. People often want to talk about their interests and are excited for new people who want to help!

▶ If you're not sure about an organization, you can check Charity Navigator.org to review the health of a nonprofit's financials.

▶ Ask in local Facebook groups (At your own risk . . . they can be helpful. You just have to use discernment.) or seek local organizations referenced in news articles.

Strengthen your friendships:

▶ Turn loose connections into strong ones through shared interests. Say yes to meeting someone's friend of a friend, and don't be afraid to bring your own friends along.

▶ If you're getting more involved with politically interested friends, start a civic group chat. Keep in touch by sharing news, venting about headlines, and turning things like meetings and volunteering into social events. Host debate-watching and election night parties. Invite your new friends to go door-knocking or to a postcard-writing party. Almost anything can be a party with the right attitude and beverages.

Filling your cup:

▶ Self-care, had it not been conceptually mangled by social media, is inherently political, and civic engagement can be self-care. The origins of radical self-care are credited to Black feminist writer Audre Lorde, who used the terminology to assert the autonomy of Black women and as an act of appreciation, self-acceptance, and self-preservation to continue the fight for equality and resources.[1]

▸ When it comes to making self-soothing choices about how to engage, this means going to speaking events where you are empowered to make change, where you are inspired by the group and activities rather than drained. Finding comfortable spaces with like-minded people is a way to feel less alone in your world-views and supported by community.

When you finish this exercise, go to page 183, "Bringing It All Together," and write down a few notes.

How to Lobby Elected Officials Without Spending a Dollar

FROM YOUR LOCAL SCHOOL BOARD to the halls of Congress, you and your community already have the tools and power to effect change. The key words of that last sentence being *you and your community*. The status quo isn't going to change itself, and it's going to take a lot of collective effort. More people engaged in that effort means reducing the individual burden on each of us. It's important to stay aware of when and which things are happening at various levels of government, and to build a network of friends who will keep you motivated, accountable, and in the know.

For example, let's say you're personally invested in and passionate about funding programs for legislation to protect people with disabilities. Get involved with a relevant nonprofit, follow people on social media who focus on this area, and share with like-minded friends. These are all steps that will put you in a prime position to act when it matters. If a bill comes up for a floor vote in Congress to strengthen enforcement of the Americans with Disabilities Act, you'll be the first to know that it's time to call your representatives' offices to let them know how strongly you'd support their YES vote on that bill. Don't worry about calling them too many times. This is their chance to win over another volunteer or donor for their next reelection campaign. Would a store turn away a customer?

STEP 1: PICK YOUR FAVORITE SOLUTION(S)

We've talked a lot elsewhere about figuring out what issue you want to work on. However when you contact or meet with your representative, the key is to have a specific ask. Don't just say "fix the healthcare system" but have a particular bill number, legislative action item you want them to do (e.g., vote in favor), or policy changes you want to see.

The fastest way to identify a specific legislative action item to advocate for is to find an organization or social media account that focuses on the issue you care about and see what bills they are advocating for. As discussed further in the Additional Resources lesson 6, the policy-making process is rife with opportunities for input. This could be pushing for bill co-sponsorship, a committee hearing, a floor vote or more. Connecting with experts who are following the day-to-day process on the bill is a great way to find out exactly what action item to work on.

Even without that specificity, pushing for passage of bills you care about is always a good thing. On the local level, you might have a specific outcome already in mind (e.g., add a traffic light at the intersection in front of the school) that you can bring to your town council or mayor.

STEP 2: RESEARCH YOUR REPRESENTATIVE

Who has the power to fix your favorite problem? Is it state or federal? Find the person or people who need your vote to keep their job, and these are the people you should reach out to. The smaller the district, the more responsive they will be to your concerns. For example, if you want to impact a decision being made by the Food and Drug Administration, you don't call the FDA, you call your members of Congress and ask them to push the FDA to do something (by signing a letter, passing legislation, or asking questions at a hearing).

If you are calling someone in Congress, they have two offices you can reach out to. First is their D.C. office, and second is their in-state office that is closest to you. We recommend saving these numbers in your phone. Adding to favorites even.

STEP 3: CHOOSE YOUR METHOD OF CONTACT

Option A: Call

Phone calls are an extremely effective way to influence your legislators because they know it takes effort to make a phone call, implying that you care a lot. An email or text can be sent through an automated system, but if you're willing to make a call it means you really care and are paying attention. When they receive *a lot* of phone calls on a particular issue, they're more likely to take notice or potentially change their vote on something. This dynamic is emblematic of the average age of our lawmakers.

Most offices tally the calls daily—which means they keep track of how many people called in favor or against an issue, or the number of people who called to ask the office to cosponsor a bill. You don't need to go into detail, but framing what you want in specific legislative terms is most effective. Most of the time the staffer will thank you and tally. Don't feel the need to do a lot of prep, you are not going to have to defend or get into a back and forth on substance with the office.

A Script for Calling Your Representatives

Introduction: "Hello, my name is [*Your Name*], and I'm a constituent from [*Your Town*]. I'm calling to discuss [*Your Issue*]."

Your Stance: "I believe that [*Express Your Opinion on the Issue*]."

Ask for Support: "I'm calling to ask [*Representative's Name*] to [*Your Ask from Step 1*]."

Thank You: "Thank you for your time. This issue means a lot to me."

Option B: An Email

Political advocacy organizations often have easy-to-use email templates available on their websites or social media accounts, but if you can't find one, use this template anytime you want to quickly send an email based on an issue you care about.

A Template for Emailing Your Representatives

Email Subject: Either include a bill's name or number. Do *not* send it with (no subject).

Introduction: Introduce yourself as a constituent and the issue you are writing about.

Body: Explain why the issue is important to you and your community.

Request: Clearly state what you'd like your representative to do.

Closing: Thank your representative for their time.

Option C: A Meeting

While it may seem intimidating or completely out of reach, you can set up a meeting with your representatives about any issue that's important to you. At the local level you can likely get a meeting with the elected officials themselves. The higher the elected office, the more levels of staff they have, but meeting with staff is still important and can be very effective.

You can go by yourself, you can go as part of an organized advocacy group, or you could even do this as an activity with the friends you've cultivated as part of your civic network.

Your representatives have offices in the district and employ staffers, known as constituent liaisons, whose job it is to have conversations with people like you. You can set up a phone, video, or in-person meeting with them. For meetings like this, it's always helpful to prepare in advance.

A personal story: Why is this important to you, and how will your representative's actions affect you? Most likely, this will be the reason you care about something enough to contact your representative in the first place.

A specific request: What are you asking them to do that is within their power?

Follow-up plan: Meeting with an official's office gives you a new access point. How are you going to keep in touch with the office? Also, if they do what you want, make sure to tell everyone you know about it. This is positive reinforcement to get them to do more things you ask them to.

Many elected officials have town halls, open office hours, or other public events where you can go and talk to them. Bring your questions and don't be afraid to say what you want. Remember, you are technically their boss! One of potentially thousands or millions, but still their boss.

STEP 4: FOLLOW UP

▸ Post on social media recommending that your friends take the same action.

▸ Make a note to follow up with your representative's office if you don't hear back within a reasonable time frame.

▸ Keep track to see if the elected official appears to be doing anything they promised (if they promised). Keep calling. Be annoying. This is your outlet. What are they gonna do, tweet about you? Screen your calls?

▶ Many times, lawmakers' offices will return a form answer to you. That doesn't mean that it's the last time you're allowed to contact them. You don't have to stop asking about the issue until they've done something.

▶ Especially at the federal level, the legislative process takes a long time; it's critical to be persistent but maintain a pace that is sustainable for you. Having hope but managing your expectations is a difficult balance. (That's why we suggest building community to share in this burden and working on local projects that move faster as well!).

▶ Escalate! If you started with an email, the next step is a phone call. Build a community to join in the calls, then request a meeting.

▶ Politicians, like all of us (and our dogs), are best trained with positive reinforcement. Even if an office doesn't do everything you asked for, a thank-you call, an op-ed in a local newspaper, or a public social media post can serve as encouragement for them to keep being responsive. Who's a good senator!?

> When you finish this exercise, go to page 184, "Bringing It All Together," and write down a few notes.

Having Challenging Conversations About Politics

ONE OF THE THINGS we discussed in earlier sections is the power of conversations to build consensus and turn around the polarization in our political discourse. We're not saying that a single conversation can save democracy, but we do believe that more conversations about these issues are important to regaining control over the civic discourse. People frequently tell us how empowered they feel once they start talking about issues they care about, and how it inspires them to do more.

Conversations about politics in these unprecedented times can be about as comfortable as initiating a divorce. We are not suggesting you start a conversation with your volatile uncle Billy at the Thanksgiving table. But there are lots of people you talk to on a regular basis—your mom or dad, your friend from the day-care pickup line, your coworker's husband at a dinner party—who might be interested in having these conversations. You might be surprised how many people out there have a political issue they are secretly passionate about.

The more political conversations you have, the more confident you will be. This is a foundational skill for the work of advocacy, power building, and political change—building coalitions of people who support your ideas and share your values.

Here are some of our favorite tips:

Shared or Special Interests Are an Easy Starter: Finding a common ground to begin the conversation, or just figuring out what the other person cares about, is the easiest way to start a conversation. *Oh, your daughter also goes to Riverdale High; are you worried about the library changes?*

Follow Up with Open-Ended Questions: When you don't know what to say next, the easiest move is a tell-me-more. *How did you hear about this? Who else is involved?*

Listen Actively: Show that you're paying attention by nodding, paraphrasing, and asking follow-up questions. Don't look at your phone, despite how tempting it may be—and even if it's to find something to make your point. At the end of the day, many political conversations are about emotions and wanting to be heard, and that's okay. There's no requirement to reach consensus or agreement in a conversation.

Avoid Personal Attacks: If you want to keep communication lines open beyond this conversation, keep your focus on the issues you're discussing, not the person you're speaking to. *This is a really complicated issue.* [As opposed to: *You're brainwashed by disinformation.*] (If someone is treating you like trash, get away from that conversation!)

Set the Frame, Don't Just Respond to It: Define the conversation in your terms, don't feel compelled to react to others' framing. When people ask us questions it's easy to feel boxed in, but you can pivot to answer the question or respond any way you please!

Don't Overuse Negations: What you negate is what you state. This is a trick of political communications, and especially important for social media conversations. Repeating something just reinforces the very idea you're trying to argue against, and keeps the conversation framed on their terms. "When someone says "don't think of an elephant" all you can think of is an elephant. Said another way: say what you are for, not what you are against. *For example, if you were campaigning against school vouchers: instead of "say no to school choice" use the message "all kids deserve access to high quality education."*

Seek to Understand, Not to Win: The goal of most political conversations should be to learn from each other, determine if you have shared values, and build relationships, not to score points. A lot of us have been pulled into conversations over the years by people who view it as a rhetorical game. This isn't productive, because you'll never convince someone during an argument (believe us, we've tried). You will most likely just force them into a further calcified position. The goal should always be to share information, ideas, and new ways of thinking about an issue. (When you disagree! Which you might not always with your conversation partner.)

Avoid Absolutes: Phrases like "always" and "never" can be polarizing, and are usually inaccurate. Speaking in more nuanced terms can lead to a more productive dialogue.

HELPFUL PHRASES TO
DE-ESCALATE HEATED CONVERSATIONS:

"I hear you": This acknowledges someone's perspective without committing to agreement.

"Tell me more": This invites the other person to elaborate without interjecting your own opinion. It's a great way to gain more insight into their thinking and, more important, *why* they believe what they do.

"I understand where you're coming from": Even if you don't agree, acknowledging that you see their point of view can foster a more positive discussion.

"That's an interesting perspective": A diplomatic way to respond when you think you may have just uncovered an uncharted level of idiocy.

"Can you help me understand what you mean by that?": Instead of directly challenging every point reflexively, you should ask for clarification to create a beat to cool things down.

"I see this is something you feel strongly about": I'm not getting into an argument about this right now.

"Let's come back to this": If things are getting too heated, suggesting a break or changing the subject can prevent escalation.

"I need to think about that": If you're not sure how to respond or simply just ready to go home, it's best to say you need time to reflect. Let them think they convinced you if you need to. When they go low, we go high.

Tips on Raising Children with a Heart for Civic Engagement

FOR SO MANY PEOPLE, the core of their civic engagement is a desire to build a better future for their kids. Part of that is raising kids who will continue to engage in civic life. Both of our moms were integral in sparking our own political engagement, and without their inspiration, we probably wouldn't be where we are today. We know you're already busy with all the tasks of parenting, so figuring out how to involve your kids in this type of community building is also a great way to fit it into your life in a sustainable way.

Engage in Meaningful Conversations: Talk to your kids about current events and listen to their opinions. Reflect their values back to them, showing them how their daily actions relate to broader social values.

Include Them in Civic Activities: Take your kids along to events like canvassing, voting, phone banking, town halls, school board meetings, or (safe) protests.

Discuss Current Events Together: Watch and talk about the news or social media content by elected officials when appropriate.

SAMI SAGE & EMILY AMICK

Volunteer Together: Choose a political or community cause to volunteer for as a family, explaining why it matters (e.g., if your child likes animals, you can collect towels for a local animal shelter).

Create Awareness Posters: Encourage your kids to design posters about an issue they care about or candidates you want to support, and place them in your community. (We love a yard sign!)

Teach About Voting: Use games or role-play to teach them about the voting process and why it's important (e.g., vote for which movie you are going to watch).

Read Books About Civic Responsibility: Share books that relate to government, citizenship, and community service suitable for their age. (There are so many great social media accounts offering suggestions on these type of books.)

Visit Historical Sites: Plan family trips to historical sites or museums that can offer context and understanding of the nation's political history. (Kids may disagree on this one.)

Write Letters to Elected Officials: Help your kids write letters or emails to local representatives about issues that matter to them. Yes! Kids can contact their reps even though they don't vote. Sami's grandmother encouraged her to do this when she was eight years old. She distinctly recalls asking for there to be "no more guns and bombs" (she's still asking) and received a letter back. Then she kept asking if the letter was *really* from Bill Clinton, until her grandma admitted it was probably a form letter.

Create a Family Voting Tradition: If possible, make voting a family outing where kids can witness the process and celebrate our civic privilege together. (Who doesn't love an "I Voted" sticker?!)

Encourage School Participation: Support their involvement in student government or community projects at school. (We'd make a Tracy Flick joke, but we recently rewatched *Election* with Reese Witherspoon and it's not what we remembered.)

Set Up a Lemonade Stand for a Cause: Help your kids set up a lemonade stand to raise money for a candidate or issue they care about. (Our friend did this and her son became very passionate about asking people if they are registered to vote.)

> When you finish this exercise, go to page 185, "Bringing It All Together," and write down a few notes.

★ CIVIC SUCCESS STORIES
PARENTING TIPS

"Model the behavior. Take your kid to vote. Make your advocacy calls in the car on the way home from school. Don't shy away from politics at the table. The more normalized civic engagement feels as a kid, the more normal it will be as an adult."

—Shelby, age 26, Shreveport, Louisiana

"I think teaching empathy and compassion is the first step. To me those qualities naturally lead to civic engagement because that is one of the most tangible ways to make a difference in other people's lives by upholding their rights."

—Jessy, age 36, Chicago, Illinois

"They can help write letters! Or go with you to the polls. Leading by example and finding ways to let them be involved is amazing."

—Amanda, age 33, Atlanta, Georgia

"I think about my kids and my family and use that as a guide to how I focus my time and energy. It is of the utmost importance to me that my kids AND every child have the right to be their full selves. I see this as a community thing. We have a long way to go! My boys are white and I see it as my duty to make sure that Black and brown children have the same opportunities as my kids."

—Kate, age 38, New York

"Talk! Talk about the current issues, why it matters to you, differences in views between yourself and your partner. I'm a woman and mom who is the main breadwinner—I have two boys. They know I'm the main breadwinner. It's important to me they know why women are equal and why women should make all decisions over their bodies. We talk about everything in our house!"

—Sarah, age 47, Massachusetts

"Show them people they know are affected by community involvement and civic engagement. Explain how voting for this council member meant that the council members worked to get technology at their school or the PTA funded their field trip. Even showing kids that the library they love so much is a result of taxes created by elected officials, helps them connect to the need for involvement and local civic engagement to serve the community. Finding as many concrete examples locally as possible shows them the importance of these actions."

—Clare, age 26, Arlington, Virginia

Bringing It All Together

OVER THE COURSE of this book we've asked you to keep coming back to this section to write notes. When complete, this reveals your civic action plan! We hope this serves as a jumping-off point for building a civic life that is meaningful, sustainable, and adds joy to your life.

YOUR CIVIC ACTION PLAN

From the Initial Reflection Exercise:

1. What are the top three things you want to see changed in this country and in your local community?

_____

_____

2. How much time you want to dedicate to civic life:

_____

_____

3. What you want to add to your life (community, friendship, etc.):

FROM THE REFLECTION EXERCISE ON HOPE AND HOPELESSNESS

What are two techniques you want to implement when you are stuck in the hopelessness spiral?

FROM YOUR PERSONAL MISSION STATEMENT

Write out your three values mission statements:

_____
_____
_____
_____
_____
_____

AUDITING YOUR NEWS CONSUMPTION:

What is your plan for news consumption from these sources:

Social Media: _____
_____
_____

Subscriptions (newsletters, etc.): _____
_____
_____

Newspapers/Magazines: _____
_____
_____

Television: _____
_____
_____

Other: _____
_____
_____

CREATING YOUR CIVIC CALENDAR

When is your next primary? When is your next election? What are the top three calendar events you want to add to your life? (e.g., school board, campaign events for a specific politician, advocacy groups, bowling leagues, food kitchen, etc.).

_____
_____
_____
_____
_____
_____
_____
_____
_____

What steps do you need to take to fully execute this part of the plan?

_____
_____
_____
_____
_____
_____
_____
_____

BUILDING A CIVIC NETWORK
WITHOUT "NETWORKING"

What are your three goals for building a civic network?

_____
_____
_____

What are three things you are going to do to achieve those goals?

_____
_____
_____

_____
_____
_____
_____
_____
_____
_____
_____
_____
_____
_____
_____

LOBBYING ELECTED OFFICIALS
WITHOUT SPENDING A DOLLAR

1. Do you know all your elected representatives from most local to national and where they stand on the issues that are important to you? ☐ *Yes* ☐ *No*

2. What is one political issue you want to contact your representative about?

_____
_____

3. Who are the officials you want to contact? How?

RAISING CHILDREN WITH
A HEART FOR CIVIC ENGAGEMENT
(if you have kids)

What are three things you are going to do with your kid(s)?

FINAL REFLECTION EXERCISE

If you complete the steps outlined in your civic action plan, how do you think your life will be different?

What are you most hopeful for:

Personally _____

_____

_____

_____

_____

_____

_____

_____

Politically _____

_____

_____

_____

_____

_____

_____

_____

SECTION 6:
THE FUTURE IS WRITTEN BY US, NOT IN THE STARS

MANY OF THE MOST EFFECTIVE changemakers and inspiring public figures have come into their roles by circumstance, and often not good ones. Most people don't look at politics or the government and think, *Wow, such a functional and exemplary domain. Sign me up to be part of that!* It's much more likely that an advocate has witnessed or experienced a problem, a community underserved, or a crisis ignored and they felt called to step up.

People often need to be asked to run for office. They need to be asked to testify at a school board hearing. They need to be asked to serve on a nonprofit board. So this is us asking you.

We think you already have all the innate qualities you need to get started, but your most powerful tools are your voice and your choice of how to use it. If money gets to have a voice, so do you. Your lived experience, your unique perspective, the values you hold, and now your civic efforts are necessary to help build a thriving representative democracy that functions in our collective interests.

The status quo won't fundamentally change if just a few of us step up. The power of our time and energy works only at scale. The capitalists in the back know what we mean (we see you're still here). And the good news is that the more social capital we build, the stronger our social cohesion and trust, the more robust our community networks, the happier and healthier we're all more likely to be, statistically.

Throughout this book, you've drilled down on your values, devised plans to refine your news consumption, to approach creating a network of people who share your values, and to set a political calendar. (We assume you did all the activities. Were you a pleasure to have in class?) Now we just need to take action, no big deal. Unfortunately, we have no chance at realizing the future we want if we engage only in fits and starts around presidential elections. You wouldn't build a house and fill in only a quarter of the foundation. A more thoroughly representative democracy in a highly civically engaged society requires a sustained effort built from the ground up.

We hope that as you've read this book you've gained some awareness of the power that you hold to change things as well as some tips, tricks, and tools to do so. We could have written a book that claimed to offer 10 steps to destroying polarization and fixing democracy.

(Step 6: Disrupt extremism with VoteStrong bracelets!*) But the prescription for what ails America isn't a pill, it's going to require eating our vegetables. The Big Salad.

The solution to our problems is all of us, each stepping up in our own unique ways. You don't need to do everything, but we really need everyone to do something.

---

* Not a thing, a joke.

10 Rules for Political Action When We're All Very Busy and Exhausted

1. **Embrace Friction:** Don't be afraid of pushback or opposition. Being called "difficult" can be a badge of honor. If you're rubbing people the wrong way, there's a chance those people have something to lose if you achieve what you're pushing for. Like many things in life, prepare for all progress to take more time, effort, and money than you expect. If you're worried about what people will think of you, know that some will inevitably express their disapproval, but it doesn't necessarily mean you're doing anything wrong. A friend to all is a friend to none. And if you simply must consider others' opinions, remember that there will also be some people who will like you even more for being "difficult."

2. **Don't Be a Bore:** Opt for tactics that are enjoyable. Civic life shouldn't be a drag; it should unite and uplift. Much like with picking a workout routine, the best tactics are ones that you enjoy, want to keep doing, and in which others will join. That means building movements that are meaningful, connective, and positive. Humor

isn't just for jokes; it's a tool for endurance. (And an incredibly effective rhetorical weapon.) Political engagement can get heavy and acutely painful, and laughter is not only the most fun survival mechanism you can deploy, but also one of the most effective.

3. **Build Authentic Bonds:** Prioritize relationship building, not networking. It's about whom you can call to show up when there's something important going on. Shared values and genuine friendships create stronger alliances and a more fulfilling life, and in our increasingly lonely society, the act of friendship could arguably be considered political. We promise, it's worth tolerating the group chat notifications. Relationships are also a key to effective lobbying, as our entire civic infrastructure (government, courts, etc.) is made up of people. If you care about speed bumps in your town, get to know the mayor's staffer who covers road issues. Building and leveraging connections is one of the most underrated tools we have.

4. **Mix It Up:** Don't let your strategies go stale; adapt and evolve. For example, petitions used to have a huge impact, but politicians have become immune to that advocacy device because they've realized how limited people's follow-through is once they've signed a petition. It also gets boring for you and the people you want to join in. To keep the energy high and ideas fresh, add new people, issues, or methods to the mix. Commit to diversifying the perspectives (and of course the people) around you to keep your work fresh and engaging. Staying cutting-edge doesn't mean jumping on every trend, but it does mean being willing to change and adapt for long-term efficacy.

5. **Listen and Learn:** Building intersectional movements where the majority bands together to take back power from an overrepresented minority requires listening and learning from the people in your coalition. Playing politics also generally means listening to people with other stakes in the negotiations to find common ground and a path forward. There is so much to learn from people who have done this work before you, from how to phrase a question (maybe a school board official has a favorite coffee shop, and if you ask for a meeting there, you're more likely to get it) to what has already been tried and failed (and why!).

6. **Build Power:** Being right gets you a gold star, but building power gets you wins and change. The brass tacks of political organizing and advocacy involves creating structures and campaigns that can influence or replace elected officials. Even when it comes to the judiciary, those people are either elected or nominated by elected officials, which means that the buck always comes back to the voter. You may be saying to yourself, I just want to make phone calls—but you still get to decide what group you're making those calls with, whom you're calling, and what you are calling about. This is about mindset inasmuch as it's about tactics; if you want to see a small change, you need small power; if you want to see a big change, you need big power.

7. **Storytelling as Strategy:** Humans have used storytelling for millennia to teach lessons, pass on history, and build community. What drives people is emotions (this isn't news to anyone who's seen which videos on social media get the most views and clicks). Stories transform policy ideas into digestible narratives that illustrate the

real-world impact of political decision-making. Whether you are talking to a neighbor or a candidate, it's effective to relay an individual narrative or inspiration to galvanize action.

8. **Slow, Steady, and Consistent Wins the Races:** Forget instant gratification. For that, try a microwave dinner. The most impactful movements simmer over time, gathering momentum and dedicated grassroots support. Online clicktivism has made people feel like they can be part of something in an instant, which is not inherently a bad thing, but the problem is that the interest often doesn't go beyond the click. The reality is that significant civic movements that have been able to achieve *major* changes are ones that built slowly and, to be frank, painfully. It's much easier to block than it is to make change, and substantial progress often requires replacing the decision-makers (judges, politicians, etc.). For so many of us, politics is a biannual freakout instead of a daily habit, but most progress you want to see will require years of sustained effort. The good news is that the sooner more of us get involved, the less time it should take.

9. **Make Room for Ebb and Flow:** A tree doesn't blossom in every season. Bears are hardly even conscious in every season. Nothing can grow infinitely forever. Every actor has their better and their weaker roles, with the exception of Meryl Streep. The same applies to the cycles of civic life. Certain issues will take priority at certain times, and if everything is an emergency, then nothing is. There are times to make progress behind the scenes, and there are times to spread that work widely in public and sustainably broaden your

cause. And sometimes the seasons of *your* life mean you need to take a step back. Periods of relative quiet provide a moment to gain perspective, conceive new ideas, and help you feel refreshed for the next big season of getting things done.

10. **Pop the Champagne:** Celebrate your wins, no matter how small. It fuels morale to reward your efforts. Negativity doesn't do anything to speed up progress, it just makes people less likely to enjoy hanging out with you. Systemic change is often the result of persistent, incremental efforts. Don't wait for the big moment—it may never come.

SECTION 7:
ADDITIONAL RESOURCES

Book Club Discussion Guide

ONE WAY to build a civic community is to host a book or article club. For a first meeting, we'd encourage you to invite your civically curious friends to a *Democracy in Retrograde* book club (and maybe ask them to invite one person each). The goal of this book is to start these conversations between you and yourself, but we hope this discussion guide will enable you to later ignite conversations in your civic pod.

You could also arrange to write postcards or send emails to your elected officials at this party! We'd love to hear more on social media about what your agenda was for your *DIR* book club!

A CONVERSATION ABOUT THE BOOK:

1. Sami and Emily make the case that democracy is in retrograde, citing, in particular, the issue of minority rule. Is this something you've thought about before, and do you agree that this is a serious issue in America?

2. Polarization, calcification, and tribalization are treated as three different trends. Have you noticed these trends in your

day-to-day life, and do you think there's something particular to American democracy that reinforces these issues?

3. The "public square" was a literal place in communities for most of human existence. It's now mostly virtual. How have the changes in our society and culture changed the value and promise of the public square? Do you see it as useful in modern life?

4. "Social capital" is defined as the connections between people that bind communities together. Is it possible to rebuild social capital in our modern era? What are some practical methods or strategies to achieve this?

5. Do you think the "Exhausted Majority" is a real thing? Do you identify with that as part of this category?

6. British anthropologist Robin Dunbar said that our brains can handle only 150 relationships. Do you think you make contact with that many people in your regular life? What about if you count social media or tech-only relationships?

A CONVERSATION ABOUT YOURSELVES:

1. How have you been feeling about politics in recent years?

2. Do you see a distinction between civic engagement, community life, and politics? What is it?

3. What is your hope outlook? Did the hope outlook framework help you gain any insight into how you've been approaching political issues?

4. Which civic personality did you score the highest on? Do you feel that it fits you? Do you find it challenging to categorize yourself?

5. Do you feel that you have a place in the political process? Do you feel confident advocating for issues you care about? Why or why not?

6. What do you think is holding you back from getting involved?

7. Do you have many political conversations in your day-to-day life? Why or why not? Were you surprised by the research finding that conversations that result in consensus actually change people's brains? (They "click" together.)

8. Do you feel that you incorporate activities, people, and/or causes that are reflective of your personal values into your life on a regular basis? If not, what do you think you need to change about your life?

A CONVERSATION ABOUT YOUR POLITICAL INTERESTS:

1. What are your top-priority political issues, and why? Which people or groups are most impacted by the issues you chose? Are they different, or are all your chosen issues impacting the same, or overlapping, groups of people?

2. How do these political issues reflect the values you laid out in your personal mission statement? Are they aligned?

3. Are your priority issues local or federal? Have you been able to connect specific action items to each? What are they?

4. In what ways and to what extent do you feel these political issues affect you personally?

A CONVERSATION ABOUT NEXT STEPS:

1. Is everyone willing to share their next steps in their civic action plan?

2. What are your favorite "third spaces" that you want to start visiting more (places that people can spend time together, like parks, libraries, and clubs)?

3. What dates have you saved in your civic calendar?

4. Which organizations are you excited to get more involved in?

5. What are some news sources that you find the most helpful, or have you noticed any accounts whose credibility (or lack thereof) has earned them an unfollow?

6. Are we aware of all our elected officials, from local to national?

7. What are your biggest hurdles or challenges in implementing your civic action plan?

How the Government Works

LESSON 1
Are We a Democracy or a Republic?

* * *

You may be wondering how we can be asking such a question in our pro-*democracy* book. This is more a question of the colloquial way we use the term "democracy," but it's also evolved into a favored talking point of internet trolls (and their real-world tethers). They love to say that the United States isn't even *supposed* to be a democracy, it's a republic. Not since 12th-grade government class have you heard this point delivered so pompously.

Here's what's really going on: those who try to build a straw man out of the fact that we aren't a "direct democracy" are doing so as intellectual scaffolding for their actual goal, which is that we *shouldn't try to be more of one.* Notice how becoming a *more representative* democracy is hardly ever the agenda that comes in the wake of ye olde democracy vs. republic distinction. That's because those who tend to bring it up are typically trying to justify *reducing* representation further by saying: *our country isn't a democracy anyway, so you can't be mad when I support policies that will make us even less of one.*

> **Mike Lee** ✔
> @SenMikeLee
>
> We're not a democracy.
>
> 9:34 PM · Oct 7, 2020

We chose to address this here because it's not just a conversation in fringe corners of the internet, but was publicly stated in 2020 by Utah senator Mike Lee (a former clerk to Supreme Court Justice Samuel Alito). By that, Senator Lee meant that we are not a direct democracy.[2] In a direct democracy, every citizen has a vote on every ballot decision. Imagine if every bill, every law, every congressional rule had to be voted on by every voter in the United States. Absolute chaos.

The suggestion that to be deemed a democratic government requires a one-to-one direct democracy is a hollow argument that's used to justify consolidating minority rule rather than striving for more proportional representation. Beyond that, noted intellectual snob Mike Lee should already know that no civilization has ever governed as a *true* direct democracy, and that the closest model was Athens in the fifth century BCE, when "citizens" gathered to vote in person. Who were these citizens? Only the adult males who weren't enslaved, which left only 10–20 percent of the Athenian population. Or did you think it was just a coincidence that every single statue to come out of the "Cradle of Democracy" looks like the exact same guy?

In the United States, we operate as what's known as a democratic republic. This means that we, the people, elect individuals

> "A republic, if you can keep it."
>
> —BENJAMIN FRANKLIN

to represent our interests and make decisions on our behalf through their votes while in elected office. This arrangement was drawn from the Roman Republic, where a Senate was chosen to govern, providing a buffer between the people and the power to make laws.

LESSON 2
The Nesting Dolls of Government: Local, State, and National

* ★ *

A big debate among the Founding Fathers was whether the yet-unformed federal government or the existing individual state governments should have more power. The former is referred to as pro-federalism, and the latter as pro–states' rights. In the end, they decided on a balance that leaned in favor of federalism, but vaguely delineated in the Constitution the rights of each, and where one could not infringe on the other.

As a result, the fabric of American governance is a multilayered structure that allows for diverse and specific representation, which is meant to be more responsive and tailored to our heterogeneous population and distinctive communities. The way things are done varies widely among states, counties, cities, and towns, but generally follows the same hierarchy.

The layers of our government are sort of like Russian nesting dolls. You pick one up and open it to discover even smaller elected officials hidden inside one another (and sometimes, one another's pockets). Each layer has its own responsibilities, yet they all fit together to form a complete set of the people *we* voted for to get things done on our behalf.

Local Government: Cities, towns, municipalities, villages. These are where decisions about schools, parks, roads, libraries, and local ordinances are made. They are the most directly accessible to the individual citizen, both in terms of where to access resources and/ or to run for public office.

County Government: In many states, counties carry significant roles in judicial functions, law enforcement, and managing public health matters.

State Government: The state creates laws and allocates funding for education, transportation, and commerce within its borders, wielding a broad array of functions that differ from state to state. While enjoying broad powers under the 10th Amendment, state governments are restricted by federal law in areas such as civil rights and interstate commerce. Each state functions as an independent sovereign entity within the scope of their powers and has their own constitutions, court systems, and law enforcement. The relationship between federal and state law is complex, often leading to legal battles in areas where their respective jurisdictions might overlap.

Federal Government: The federal government regulates matters that span the entire nation, such as foreign policy, defense, and federal taxation, as well as things that affect "interstate commerce" (i.e., business that takes place in multiple states). Often the federal government will use money as a mechanism to control state policy. For example, a state will get funding if they do X, or won't get it if they do Y. Ultimately, the Supremacy Clause of the Constitution asserts that federal law reigns supreme over state law, meaning that when state and federal laws conflict, the answer is always to follow federal law.

FEDERAL & STATE TUG-OF-WAR

States have broad powers to regulate within their borders (criminal law, family law, and commerce that doesn't cross state lines), but it's not absolute. The 10th Amendment says that any powers not delegated to the federal government are reserved to the states, which accounts for *a lot*. As a result, the entity really in control of a matter tends to get murky in practice.

A demonstrative example of how this works is education policy, which is technically considered a state power. States create school districts and set curriculum standards, and individual localities (such as towns and villages) are big financial contributors to funding schools through property tax revenue (and therefore, one of the drivers of the major chasm between public school offerings in the U.S.). The federal government also provides massive amounts of funding and resources on top of what the states do.

This reliance on a portion of education funding from the federal government leaves room for it to exert influence through congressional legislation and executive powers (i.e., the President and the Department of Education). Within the federal government, the DOE is responsible for things like funding early childhood education, programs for kids with disabilities, collecting data and ensuring that schools across the country are complying with constitutional guidelines like antidiscrimination laws.

As convoluted as governance in the United States tends to be, the complexity is part of the design and was intended to maintain balance. The system was set up so progress would require time and broad consensus. However, the present circumstances of extreme gridlock and polarization have reached what authoritarian scholars agree are red-alert levels.[3] A slow-rolling minority takeover was not the idea behind designing our country's laws to evolve slowly.

As frustrated as you are that certain progress can't be made, fellow Americans whose idea of progress is the exact opposite of yours probably feel the same on their end. So be careful how fast you wish the system would allow for change, because that could mean change in the opposite way you want.

Present issues aside, our point stands that the slow speed isn't inherently a bad thing on its own. The problem is when there is *no* speed, especially on urgent issues where Americans agree. Federalism allows states to act as mini-democracies, experimenting with different policies and approaches that reflect their individual cultures and needs. Simultaneously, it ensures a unifying framework that holds the states together as one. Can't you feel the oneness?

LESSON 3
The Constitution and the Three Branches of Government

* ★ *

When it comes to the final say of how things are "supposed" to work, the Constitution was intended to serve as a road map, designating specific powers to different levels and branches of government. This structure is designed, theoretically, to limit any one entity from taking control.

Before the amendments that comprise the Bill of Rights, the Constitution lays out the three articles that delineate the three branches of government, with additional amendments coming after.

The first three articles outline the functions and limitations of the legislative, executive, and judicial branches within the federal government. To prevent any confusion, the division of powers between the three branches is an entirely separate matter from the division of state and federal power. Everything in the following section (until the big header "State and Local Politics," you can't miss it) is about the federal government, and all federal branches supersede state government.

Legislative Branch (Congress): Article I grants Congress the power to make laws, collect taxes, declare war, and oversee other areas of federal policy.

Executive Branch (The President): Article II vests the President with the executive power, defining roles in enforcing laws, leading the military, and managing foreign affairs.

Judicial Branch (Federal Courts): Article III establishes the federal judiciary, giving it the authority to interpret and apply the law in federal cases. The federal judiciary is distinct from the federal criminal justice system, in that it is primarily concerned with interpreting and ruling on the constitutionality of legislation and actions by *both* federal and state governments. The hierarchy of the judiciary goes (in ascending order of authority): State Supreme Courts → District Courts → Circuit (aka Appeals or Appellate) Courts → the Supreme Court.

THE LEGISLATIVE BRANCH

The legislative branch is composed of two distinct and complementary bodies: the Senate and the House of Representatives, which together are referred to as Congress. Congress is the only federal body with the power to pass laws. The framers of the Constitution aimed to balance various interests and protect the rights of both the individual states and the people by creating two houses with different purposes, members, and modes of operation.

The House of Representatives

The House of Representatives is the most "democratic" body in federal government, with 435 members divided among the states in proportion to their respective populations, giving more populous states more representatives. However, the total number of congressional representatives hasn't increased since 1929, when that number was capped at 435 by the Permanent Apportionment Act, even though the country's population has ballooned since. According to the 2020 census, each district represents 761,169 people. Compare this with 1930, when each district represented only 280,675 people.[4] Members of the House serve only two-year terms, which means that they have to campaign every other year to keep their job, so they're constantly trying to raise money for reelection.

The House's exclusive powers include initiating revenue bills and impeaching (but not convincing) federal officials. It was, in theory, designed to be more responsive to the people, with frequent elections allowing for rapid shifts in representation in response to changes in public sentiment.

The Senate

The Senate consists of 100 members: two from each state, irrespective of the state's population. As elderly as possible, please. Senators serve six-year terms, with one-third of the seats up for election every two years. This structure was established by the Great Compromise of 1787, after the less populous states were afraid that they'd be constantly overlooked in a congressional body where they're outnumbered, as the House was designed.

The Senate's unique responsibilities include ratifying treaties, confirming presidential appointments (e.g., federal judges and cabinet members), and conducting impeachment trials. Its design and responsibilities reflect the need for an entity that can act with deliberate wisdom, as they're somewhat insulated from the rapid fluctuations of public opinion due to the their longer terms in office. We'd argue they have achieved that in spades.

THE EXECUTIVE BRANCH

The executive branch has the responsibility of implementing and enforcing laws, as well as managing the day-to-day affairs of the government. This branch is headed by the President, which is what most people associate with the executive branch, but the phrase also encompasses the full administration and its Cabinet, including the agencies run by each secretary. Those Cabinet agencies are essentially granted their powers as an extension of the President. The authority granted to the executive branch under the Constitution by Article II, Section 2, is vast yet somewhat restrained.

Presidential Powers

Commander-in-Chief: The President leads the nation's military and can respond to immediate threats. In theory, the War Powers Resolution of 1973 requires the President to consult with Congress if military engagement exceeds 60 days, while Congress also controls the purse (aka the budget), so they are the ones who decide how much funding goes to defense/wars. In practice, this gets blurry in the era of modern warfare. The authorizing resolution passed by Congress to allow the invasion of Afghanistan has been used at least 41 times to engage in conflicts in 19 countries.[5]

Treaty Negotiation: The President can negotiate treaties, subject to the Senate's approval, which requires a two-thirds majority. This negotiation is often done through a team at the Department of State, which is an executive branch agency.

Appointments: The President nominates federal judges, ambassadors, and cabinet members. These appointments require Senate confirmation. The appointment of judges and justices, who have lifetime terms, is one of the strongest powers held by the President. What's less often discussed is that the executive branch also appoints thousands of people to work in agencies across the government. In general, the various agencies of government are staffed by a combination of career civil service workers and politically appointed officials who come and go by administration.

Veto Power: The President can veto bills passed by Congress, though a veto can be overridden by a two-thirds majority vote in both the House and Senate.

Executive Powers: Presidents can issue executive orders and, through federal departments and agencies, they can also issue rules, regulations, policy interpretations, and other administrative actions. Executive orders are one way that a President can shape policy, but they are not technically laws. Only Congress can pass laws. Executive orders are also still subject to review by federal courts. While an executive order can't create a completely new law, that doesn't mean it can't have a strong practical impact. An executive order can be used to outline how to enforce existing laws (or not, in the case of marijuana decriminalization, for example), or to manage the staff and resources of the executive branch to a particular end. If you ever think that these seem like a half measure, that may often be the case, but we'll note that the Emancipation

Proclamation, which declared an end to slavery in Confederate states in 1863, was an executive order.

Pardons: The President can pardon someone from a federal, but not a state, crime. A distinction that has become more relevant as of late.

Executive Agencies:
The Workhorses of Federal Government

There are dozens of agencies in the federal government, and it can be hard to keep track of them. For the uninitiated news follower, this is one of those areas where eyes start to glaze over, just as they might watching a congressional committee that is seemingly always up to both something and nothing.

There are some agencies you've probably heard of (like the Department of Transportation) and some you maybe haven't (like the National Highway Traffic Safety Administration, which is part of the Department of Transportation). Many are tied to positions in the President's Cabinet (State Department, Department of Labor). Some are involved in regulations we hear about all the time (like the Food and Drug Administration), while others provide essential services (the Postal Service), law enforcement (the Department of Justice, the Federal Trade Commission), national security (the Department of Homeland Security, the National Security Council, the CIA, which is staying abbreviated), and forward-thinking initiatives such as research and development (NASA, also staying abbreviated). Within agencies they have the power to create new agency rules and interpret whatever rules are currently on the books. Sometimes, Congress will pass a law and tell an agency to just figure out how to use their authority to accomplish a particular action.

The executive branch is designed to allow for decisive action when needed, while also being held in check by the other branches. This design aims to prevent the concentration of power that the Founders feared would lead to tyranny. As we know, while our young government was in its infancy, nothing loomed quite as large as the specter of King George and his fully armed battalion to remind them of his love. *Da-da-da da-da!**

THE JUDICIAL BRANCH

The third pillar of the federal government, the judiciary, serves to interpret if and how the laws passed by Congress, and the actions and decisions of the executive branch, are technically allowed (i.e., constitutional). They may be the branch that's historically had the least conspicuous touch when it comes to changing American life, but in reality, these lifetime-appointed justices are major drivers of our overall culture. And not just because their collars were briefly trendy. The decisions made by the federal courts resonate through our daily lives, touching everything from individual rights to whether the government can buy your land if they decide they need it.[6] The federal court system, established under Article III of the U.S. Constitution, consists of three main levels:

* We love *Hamilton*.

U.S. District Courts: These are the trial courts where cases are initially heard. There are 94 district courts across the U.S.

U.S. Circuit Courts of Appeals: If parties are dissatisfied with a district court decision, they can appeal to one of the 13 appellate courts, which each oversee a region of the country. They hear the appeals for cases within their jurisdictions.

The U.S. Supreme Court: This is the final arbiter of federal law. It selects a small number of cases to hear each year (a massive power in and of itself), typically ones with significant constitutional implications. Other times they will choose to rule in cases where there is a split between circuits, or ones that deal with foreign powers.

FEDERAL VS. STATE COURT SYSTEMS

The federal judicial system operates parallel to but separately from individual state judicial systems (and separately from both state and federal criminal justice systems). While federal courts are governed by federal laws and the Constitution, state judiciaries are similar, except they apply state laws and constitutions.

Federal courts have jurisdiction over cases involving federal laws, treaties, disputes between states, and disputes between people from different states (where the amount in controversy is over $75,000). State courts typically handle a much broader range of cases on nearly everything within the purview of their state laws, including most criminal matters, family law, and property disputes.

LESSON 4
You Can't Do That: Checks and Balances

★ ★ ★

We all know checks and balances are meant to ensure that no single branch of government can become too powerful. Functionally this means that each branch has distinct responsibilities, and the Constitution lays out specific mechanisms to prevent any one branch from gaining unchecked control.

Legislative Checks: Congress can impeach and remove the President, reject presidential appointments, and override presidential vetoes. It also holds the power of the purse, which controls government spending (how will you do anything if you can't pay for it?), and has the authority to regulate the judiciary.

Executive Checks: The President can veto legislation that was passed by Congress, appoint federal judges, and execute the enforcement of federal laws through cabinet agencies. The President acts as the commander-in-chief of the armed forces, the highest-ranking civilian in the military. This is a role with significant diplomatic and strategic influence, but is subject to (traditionally very flexible) congressional approval for declarations of war.

Judicial Checks: The courts interpret the Constitution and federal laws, with the Supreme Court holding the ultimate judicial authority. They can declare acts of Congress or executive actions unconstitutional.

OTHER CHECKS ON POWER

Within the broad framework of checks and balances, there are several key mechanisms that help maintain this equilibrium:

Term Limits: There are no term limits for judges who are appointed to the federal judiciary. When it comes to presidential term limits, the 22nd Amendment was ratified in 1951, limiting the President to two four-year terms, as a means of preventing indefinite control of the executive branch. We hope. Congressional terms are regulated but unlimited, with two-year terms in the House of Representatives and six-year terms in the Senate, resulting in members of the House essentially becoming perennial campaigners.

Oversight: A vague concept that can mean as little or as much as the vision and/or (willful) blindness of the overseers will allow. Technically speaking, congressional oversight includes the ability to investigate and hold hearings on actions of the other two branches. The Watergate hearings are a classic example of Congress exercising this authority to probe the President's actions.

Personnel Confirmations: The Senate's role in confirming presidential appointments ensures a shared power over key governmental positions. From Cabinet members to the Supreme Court bench, this process can be contentious, as seen in the confirmation hearings of Supreme Court Justice Brett Kavanaugh in 2018. Additionally, Congress has the power to change the rules around their own confirmation power, which is why it requires only 50 votes to confirm a Supreme Court justice and other presidential nominees, but 60 votes to pass a regular law.

Impeachment Process: Impeachment is a check on executive and judicial misconduct, in addition to bringing great moral shame upon the impeached. Can you imagine? President Andrew Johnson was impeached in 1868 for violating the Tenure of Office Act (reading through the lines: to remove a political enemy from his Cabinet). It was over a century before there was another presidential impeachment, with Bill Clinton's in 1998, and Donald Trump's doubleheader (2019 and 2021).

LESSON 5
State and Local Politics: Who Are These People?

★ ★ ★

If you've ever driven cross-country, you can witness firsthand and in quick succession how different regions of the country have vastly distinct cultural, historical, and economic characteristics. These differences are often reflected in their approaches to local governance, such as through their laws on gun control, environmental protections, and education standards.

At their most granular, municipalities (aka towns) have a set of officials that typically includes a mayor, town council, and school board, and they are each responsible for services that people interface most intimately with in their daily lives.

▶ **Mayors** set the executive agenda for a city, overseeing departments like police and public works.

▶ **Town councils** handle legislative functions, passing local ordinances and managing budgets.

▶ **School boards** govern public education within their districts, setting policies, hiring superintendents, and managing finances.

These local offices, though often overlooked, probably shape your life on the most direct level. They are involved in everything from the quality of education to the condition of roads and public spaces. The construction of sidewalks, maintenance of police forces, zoning regulations, and other municipal functions may seem mundane, but they have profound impacts on community life. If you want to make a small but significant change that affects you and your neighbors, this is the space where you'll make progress. As much as you might support them, your congressional representative probably isn't going to be able to help you get a stoplight put at the intersection nearest your house because kids like to play there. A village or town council will be the place to get that done.

One level up from municipalities are county governments (it's also possible to have both). They're like a nested doll of the state government, acting as administrative arms, particularly in rural areas where municipal governments might be sparse or nonexistent. The county's role can vary widely depending on the state and region. In some places, the county government is responsible for law enforcement, road maintenance, public health, and social services. In others, it might primarily function as a judicial administrative entity. As the most expensive attorneys say, it depends.

Take Los Angeles County, which is the most populous county in the United States and has a complex government structure responsible for various services, from public health to transportation, with a budget in the tens of billions a year. (Los Angeles, the city, also has a mayor, city council, and more.) In contrast, Connecticut dissolved county governments in 1960, with state agencies assuming most administrative responsibilities. Obviously, there's a vast size and population difference between the two, which demonstrates how customizable local government can be, for better or worse. The variety of county roles across states underscores the flexibility and adaptability of the United States' system, allowing each region to tailor its structure to the unique needs and expectations of its constituents.

Finally, we have the structure of state governments. State officials include elected and appointed positions such as governors, lieutenant governors, secretaries of state, attorneys general, and state legislators.

▶ **Governors** wield substantial influence over state policy, serving as the chief executive officers of their states, like state presidents. They have the power to sign or veto legislation, appoint officials, and oversee the state's executive branch, including some electoral processes.

▶ **Legislatures** are essentially dual-chambered mini-Congresses* within each state government that are responsible for writing and passing state laws. They interact with local governments, such as counties, in an oversight role to allocate funding. As a result, laws and decisions made by state legislatures will directly influence local policies and programs.

▶ **Attorneys general** serve a mirror function to the U.S. Attorney General but for the states. You may be sensing a theme here. They play a significant role in shaping legal interpretations of state laws, which affects how those laws are enforced in practice. They may also take part in multistate legal actions on national issues, as seen in the coalition of 20 states led by Texas attorney general Ken Paxton to challenge the Affordable Care Act in 2018.

HOW MUCH POWER DO THESE STATE LEGISLATURES ACTUALLY HAVE?

Even though all but one state legislatures mirror the two-house structure of our national Congress, the composition, structure, and function of state legislatures vary significantly. They also go by different names, which is only semantics and doesn't imply anything specific about those bodies. For example, California's State

---

* Nebraska is an exception with its unicameral legislature (one house), and the smallest state legislative branch in the country, with only 49 senators. They're also a nonpartisan legislature, which means that a candidate's political party is not listed on the election ballot. For senators to win a seat, they first run in a top-two primary, and the two candidates who obtain the most votes in the primary election then compete in a general election. Once elected, leadership in the legislature is also not based on party affiliation and there's technically no majority. One could say they really hate labels. They wouldn't last a minute in Dorit's closet.

Assembly has 80 members, while New Hampshire's House of Representatives has 400, so they have different names and sizes but serve equivalent functions in their respective states.

At the same time, the terms, qualifications, and even salaries of state legislators can differ vastly. In Texas, the legislature meets every two years, whereas New York's meets annually. Rhode Island's legislators serve part-time and are compensated with approximately $15,000/year salary. These particulars are relevant only as far as they present factors that make it either more accessible or more challenging for different demographics to realistically campaign and serve in these legislatures, based on socioeconomic and other structural realities.

Regardless of the individual challenges associated with different legislative structures, the breadth of potential for variation is the lesson here. Depending on the spaces or channels you frequent, you may occasionally hear people describe states as "laboratories of democracy." The notion of states as individual laboratories where innovative policies can be tested and refined was coined by Justice Louis Brandeis in his dissenting opinion in *New State Ice Co. v. Liebmann* (1932). He articulated the idea that a state could, if its citizens chose, "serve as a laboratory; and try novel social and economic experiments without risk to the rest of the country."

There is a compelling reason why subjects like education, transportation, and public health are often left to the states. States possess an inherent understanding of their demographics, economies, and needs. Not to mention that huge areas and groups of people can become unwieldy, which has consequences. Their localized insights enable them to enact laws that resonate with their circumstances.

ELECTION DAY EFFICIENCY: REFERENDUMS AND INITIATIVES

One thing that sets states and localities apart is their ability to use referendums and ballot initiatives, which allow residents to vote directly for a specific policy on election day. This is the closest America gets to direct democracy at work, and we are confident that this is way better than what the Athenians had going.

This is how states have recently protected abortion rights, given people with felony convictions back their right to vote, decriminalized marijuana, and more. Sometimes these will go by other terms such as ballot questions, propositions, or recall elections. There are lots of different names for it, but the idea is that there are ways for the people to organize and vote to circumvent their state legislature and pass the policies they want.

LESSON 6
Where Do Laws Come From?

* ★ *

There are a few different ways to tell the story about how something goes from an idea in someone's head to a law we're collectively required to follow. No two pieces of legislation share the same story, like the special snowflakes they are. Once there's a first draft, it needs to be ushered through various stages, from committee reviews to floor debates, then to the President's (or Governor's) desk. Each stage represents a unique set of challenges. From the spark of an idea, it embarks on a labyrinthine journey through the halls of power about which Homer could write a tale.

A BILL IS BORN

The idea for legislation can arise from a citizen's frustration, an advocacy group's cause, a corporation's interest, or (on embarrassingly rare occasions) a legislator's own vision. Typically, one source will bring an idea to a legislator (or more likely, to their staff), who will then start conferring with other relevant stakeholders. These include groups that would be impacted by the hypothetical new law, academics who can provide historical context, policy experts and executive agencies that can back up the legislation with data, and other congressional offices to see if they have constituents who would be affected by the bill. This is the stage when lawmakers seek input from advocacy groups, think tanks, corporations in the relevant industry, and the lobbyists who represent all the above, but it could also be YOU!

A BILL'S INFANCY

Aides who work in congressional offices are the people who actually make the institution run. They serve as extensions of their boss, which means they are the ones who are meeting with stakeholders, consulting lawyers on how to draft language, and liaising with other congressional offices to find cosponsors. Meanwhile, the lawmaker(s) who is the lead sponsor of the bill are tasked with working to build support behind the scenes and with getting other lawmakers to sign on as cosponsors to signal consensus, in order to increase its chances of passing. Although it's the congressional staff who do the vast majority of work, members of Congress are typically out in public with press and constituents. (And, of course, raising money.)

Once a member of Congress's office has the text of a bill they want to propose, it's sent over to an office to be "introduced." The text of the bill becomes public record on Congress.gov, where constituents can access it.

Once a bill is introduced, it's referred to a committee. Depending on which chamber it was introduced in, either the Speaker of the House or the Senate's Presiding Officer is responsible for assigning it to a committee based on the bill's subject matter. A bill can also be assigned to multiple committees; for example, if its contents are relevant to both foreign affairs and judiciary issues.

A BILL'S TODDLERHOOD

Any bill needs enough support to pass Congress, which means there need to be reasons for a majority (more than 50 percent of the House or 60 votes in the Senate) to support the bill; or somewhat more important for lawmakers to have reasons *not* to object to the bill. The House and Senate both employ nonpartisan teams of lawyers, known as legislative counsel, whose job is to draft the legislation and any amendments to it. Sometimes they are given an idea, and sometimes they are given a draft already written by outside stakeholders. Amendments could be crafted by an activist group, or it could be lifted straight from the email of a lobbyist, it's hard to say. Staff who work on congressional committees have often seen many versions of bills trying to address a topic, and they're looked to for experience on the pitfalls and possibilities of a bill.

What most people don't see, and most textbooks won't include, are the intense clashes behind the scenes between lobbyists and advocacy groups, which usually result in compromises and conditions on any given piece of legislation. This way, if on the rare occasion a bill eventually *does* pass through Congress, no one is totally happy, but everyone has accolades to pocket for use as talking points on MSNBC and Fox News during the next election. We mention this not just to clarify what is really involved in the process of making our country's policies, but because this negotiation process presents an opportunity for you to influence legislation.

A BILL'S CONTENTIOUS ADOLESCENCE

Once a bill has been assigned to a committee, it still doesn't necessarily mean that it will go up for a vote. Committee chairs, who are chosen by the majority party's leader, are the gatekeepers here. (And these choices are often based on seniority, which is why many of the committee chairs are old.) They decide which bills get hearings, which go up for a committee vote (called a markup), and which get put into the circular filing cabinet.

Sometimes representatives will want to get something inserted into moving legislation on behalf of their district or other special interests.

Committees and subcommittees have the power to conduct hearings, which are called by the all-powerful chair, and can function to conduct fact-finding, testimony collection, or merely a circus to draw public scrutiny and attention to a cause (or possibly just to themselves). You never know which C-SPAN clip might go viral. Public hearings are also intended to give citizens, experts, and other stakeholders a platform and a microphone to express their views. What topics get chosen for hearings? Who is chosen to speak at them? How much work is put into calling press attention to the hearings? These backroom decisions all shape the public conversations around policy and eventually the outcomes.

FOR FACTS' SAKE:

Senate Seniority Perks

In the Senate, each member is given funding to hire a staffer who solely staffs the committee process. The higher the ranking of a member on the committee, the more staff they can hire. These staffers can develop an expertise in specific topics.

The committee markup session is where a bill's text is amended and put up for a vote. Members of the committee can propose amendments to alter the bill, and usually these aren't surprises to the rest of the committee. If a member is offering an amendment they want to see passed, they will work behind the scenes to come up with something that will get enough votes beforehand. This could involve merely convincing others of their viewpoint or cobbling together a package that includes a little bit of something for everyone.

Often, the chair of the committee will put together something called a managers package, which is a group of amendments that will get the bill to a place where it can pass out of committee. Sometimes, these changes are minor; other times, they can drastically shift the bill's intent. Members also offer stand-alone amendments, sometimes just for messaging (to either be able to say they did it or to make the other side vote against it). If a member is offering an

FOR FACTS' SAKE:

Skipping Committee

It's important to note that there are a couple ways to sidestep the committee process. The most common is a procedure that in the Senate is called **unanimous consent**. This means that a bill is put up for passage on the floor and will automatically go through unless someone says they don't want it. This means that just one senator can hold up a bill. In some circumstances, a bill can be added as an amendment to something already on the floor.

In the House, the bill must go through the House Rules Committee before the floor, which is a process committee that decides how long it will be debated on the floor and what amendments may be offered. A bill does not have to go through other House committees before Rules, but it has to go through the Rules Committee to get onto the floor. However, there's also a process called passing rules **on Suspension** which is used to pass things like post office name changes (and some-times more) because it bypasses the Rules Committee, limits debate, and prohibits amendments. If this seems overly com-plicated, that's because it is.

amendment, they are required (by the rules of the Senate, not by law) to notify the other members of the committee beforehand.

The final stage within the committee is the vote, but this is still only a vote for the committee to approve it, not to make it a law yet. Factors that influence this decision are complex and multifac-eted. These days, party lines often dictate the voting pattern, but public opinion, interest groups, financial considerations, timing, and optics can also play a significant role.

Once a bill is voted out of committee, that's where the real struggle begins, and this is the point at which more Americans tend to become aware of a particular piece of legislation. Perhaps this process may illuminate why people feel Congress gets nothing done.

A BILL COMES OF AGE

Once a bill is passed out of its House or Senate committee it can go to the floor of its first congressional chamber for a vote, but it doesn't necessarily do so. As usual, there is a gatekeeper. The responsibility and privilege of scheduling which bills can go to the floor for a vote belongs to the Senate Majority Leader and Speaker of the House (except for in the rare instance when the Senate is 50-50, in which case it's decided by a negotiated power-sharing agreement). This scheduling isn't just a matter of timing; it's a strategic decision often influenced by political considerations, public sentiment, the whip count (aka the vote count and if they have enough votes to pass), the legislative calendar, and when they have vacations booked.

Once on the floor, bills are subject to debate and deliberation. Most bills can start in either the Senate or the House. Here, there are lots of differences between House and Senate procedures, but both procedures are set by rules made by the body itself (rules that can, therefore, be changed by them as well). Assuming the bill passes in its first chamber, it gets moved along to the second.

Before we get to THE vote, we must take a detour to the Senate. The most famous rule these days is probably the Senate filibuster.

The filibuster is the name of the procedural tactic in the Senate that is used, functionally, to raise the threshold of required votes to pass any bill from 51 to 60. Because the Senate has no timeline requirement or limit for debating a bill, the members need to first hold a vote to formally end the debate phase, and then move forward for the *actual* vote on a bill. Pause for eye rolls. This means that if there's no vote to end the debate, senators can keep debating, as long as they keep literally standing on the floor and talking to prevent a vote from taking place. If they can't end the debate, they can't pass any laws. It's the parliamentary equivalent of standing in front of a car.

This endless chattering is the actual verb action of "filibustering," which we feel compelled to spell out in case you decide to mention this topic in a casual conversation so you don't go around sounding like the civic equivalent of a stylist who can't pronounce *Loewe*. Verbiage aside, we're aware the idea of policy-making by talking until you simply can't anymore is completely absurd. But this single rule has shaped much of recent congressional policy-making.

We'll also note that the Constitution didn't intend for the Senate to have a 60-vote threshold on all bills, and the near universal usage of this tactic is a modern invention. The rule itself was created by Aaron Burr (sir) in 1806, but the first known filibuster wasn't until 1841, sparked by a debate over patronage jobs in the Senate printing office, which spiraled into a larger issue over a national banking bill.[8] The more you know.

THE BIG VOTE

Referred to officially as a floor vote, this is the vote by a full congressional chamber on whether a bill will pass. The voting itself is a highly organized process, but it includes amendments and boring procedural nonsense that may require the physical presence of all members. On some occasions, the process can be simplified to a roll call or voice vote where members are walking in and out of the room. When it comes to floor votes on major bills where passage is iffy, members who are designated as the "whips" for their party are tasked with the critical job of counting and delivering votes in real time, which can often involve last-minute negotiating and potentially new amendments. This chaotic dynamic is portrayed through Frank Underwood's role in the first season of *House of Cards*.

There are a few rules about bills that must originate in the House (for example, the Constitution says that all bills related to raising revenue must originate there), but most of the time bills can start in either chamber and then be sent over to the other for a vote. If any amendments are added during the vote in the second chamber, it then gets sent back once again to the originating chamber. For annual bills like the National Defense Authorization Act, each chamber will pass their own version, and then a conference committee is formed to reconcile the discrepancies. This committee is composed of members from both chambers and will negotiate until a unified text is achieved. This is also referred to as the reconciliation process and yields a single bill, which goes through additional voting in both chambers before being sent to the President to be signed into law.

FOR FACTS' SAKE:

Can We Get Rid of the Filibuster?

In conversations regarding the filibuster, you may occasionally hear people refer to something as the **nuclear option**. This refers to the possibility of the Senate voting to change the rules to either get rid of, or suspend, the need for a vote to end debate on a bill before the *actual* vote on it (neutralizing the filibuster and therefore the need to get 60 votes).

There have been baby steps taken in this direction. In 2013 the Democratic-led Senate removed the filibuster for all executive branch and judicial nominees other than for Supreme Court justices, in response to then–Senate Majority Leader Mitch McConnell blocking all votes on President Obama's nominees. Then in 2017 the Republican-led Senate voted to remove the filibuster for Supreme Court nominees to confirm Justice Neil Gorsuch (and later Justices Brett Kavanaugh and Amy Coney Barrett). In 2021, the Senate voted to temporarily suspend the filibuster to pass a debt ceiling hike to prevent the global economy from collapsing thanks to the stubbornness of America's most privileged nursing home.[9]

If the Senate eliminated the filibuster, it would be easier for the party in power to pass legislation with a simple majority. Opponents argue that this will make it too easy for partisans to pass legislation, as senators are now forced to reach bipartisan compromise to pass legislation with 60 votes.

The longest filibuster was by Senator Strom Thurmond, who spent 24 hours filibustering the Civil Rights Act of 1957. Infer what you will about Senator Thurmond, and the filibuster, from this information.

FOR FACTS' SAKE:

How Many Bills Does Congress Usually Pass?

Many proposed bills never make it to a floor vote. In the 116th Congress (2019–2021), 16,601 bills were introduced, but only 344 became law. In the next Congress (2021–2023), 17,817 bills were introduced while only 365 became law.[10]

Note: A "Congress" refers to a two-year session. A new Congress is started every two years, when we have a new set of elected officials. This also means that all unpassed bills from the previous Congress need to be reintroduced and all committee processes start over again. It's evident why time is of the essence for those who want to get something done, while delaying is the best tactic for those who don't.

HAPPILY EVER AFTER?

After a bill has passed both houses of Congress, the President can then sign it into law, or veto it. If there's a veto, the bill will go back to Congress to attempt to override it. Best of luck with that, as it requires a two-thirds majority in both houses, a hurdle that has been cleared only 112 times in the history of the United States, as of 2023.[11] But even once a bill is law, tomorrow is never promised. It will stay in effect as long as it's not challenged within the court system and possibly overturned by the Supreme Court ruling it unconstitutional.

The romantic notion of how a bill becomes law that we were all taught in grade school, of a piece of paper getting refined by one group, and then thoughtfully passed to another before it's finally signed by the President, is a grand simplification. The actual process is laden with complexities. Though the complicated nature of passing a law might make the process seem impenetrable, it was designed to foster consideration, debate, and ultimately, a consensus that reflects the democratic ideals of the nation. What we've seen, of course, is that money has purchased influence and expertise that have severely warped the system.

LESSON 7
How Special Interests Work the System

★ ★ ★

This may seem like a controversial statement, but the concept of lobbying is morally neutral. In a representative democracy, we're supposed to try to influence lawmakers to act on behalf of the interests of their constituents. *Lobbying* is merely the verb to describe that process and can just as easily refer to the act of calling one's representative to urge them to take a certain action.

Lobbying can be legitimately useful when experts with knowledge and experience on a particular issue help legislators write effective legislation. This can be a good thing; we want legislators looking to informed stakeholders for help. This is also where the perks of the "states as laboratories of democracy" can come in. Experts are capable of extrapolating from state policies which solutions could possibly work on a national level, and we absolutely want people with domain expertise to assist legislators in crafting data-backed policy. We just don't want that help to come from people or entities that are able to profit from the policy they're "helping" legislators craft, after first using their money to gain access to those legislators. A lot of convincing can be done over rib-eyes at an expensive D.C. steakhouse.

The core problem is that, in practice, those with money accomplish significantly more through lobbying than average citizens. For example, take the efforts of the lobbying group Pharmaceutical Research and Manufacturers of America (PhRMA) to influence Medicare prescription drug reform. Why should the people who directly benefit from high prescription costs be the most influential party in deciding how much those costs are lowered, when the purpose of Medicare is to benefit senior citizens?

There are some regulations that govern the behavior of lobbyists, who are defined as someone who spends more than 20 percent of their time on lobbying activities. Those individuals are required under a 1995 federal law, the Lobbying Disclosure Act, to register and disclose their clients, their income, and the issues they are lobbying about.[12] Since then, the law was expanded in 2018 to require lobbyists to disclose things like if they've been convicted of embezzlement. Lobbyists whose activities involve foreign sovereigns also must register under the Foreign Agents Registration Act. We'll let you be the judge of how well those regulations are working.

NEUTRALIZING THE IMPACTS OF CORPORATE LOBBYING

Public opinion, the free press, and grassroots movements are the main levers that can act as counterbalances to the power of the lobbying industry, which can both aid and obstruct legislative processes, most likely depending on what will be the most lucrative for them.

One remarkable instance of grassroots lobbying was the public's response to the Stop Online Piracy Act (SOPA) and PROTECT IP Act (PIPA) in 2011. The SOPA/PIPA protests were the first instance when people used the power of the internet to organize and advocate to Congress regarding its regulation of the internet. How meta. The bills were intended to protect against online piracy, but speech advocates from academic institutions, internet companies, and activist groups organized massive online and in-person campaigns and protests, culminating in a widespread online blackout.

This is just one example of how public opinion and media scrutiny can shape the narrative around something that lawmakers are working on, by organizing en masse to amplify voices that might otherwise be drowned out by corporate-funded lobbyists who are flush with cash and have zero degrees of separation from voting members of Congress.

As the system is built today, the most effective means of counteracting the effect of money is with mass participation on a consistent basis. And electing people we believe won't be swayed by it. The more our lawmakers are aware that we're watching (as we should, because our taxes pay their salaries), they'll be both more hesitant to vote in favor of unpopular legislation, and more fearful of losing reelection if they don't act on the issues their constituents care about.

So, remember to let your elected officials know you have your eye on them. A good public servant will take that as a challenge to turn you from a doubter into a lifelong supporter.

ACKNOWLEDGMENTS

★ ★ ★ ★ ★

THIS BOOK WOULD NOT have been possible without the dedication and support of so many people who are incredibly important to us.

First and foremost, to everyone involved in getting this book done. For our book agent, Alyssa Reuben: you made this happen, and working with you is a privilege. To our edit team at Gallery and Simon & Schuster, Lauren Spiegel and Taylor Rondestvedt, thank you for seeing the potential in this book when all we had was a cluster of ideas, extreme fear about 2024, and very little time to meet our deadlines. We are so incredibly grateful for this opportunity and for your confidence in us. To art director Lisa Litwack and Faceout Studio, we love our cover art so much and are amazed at your ability to translate our mood boards into exactly what we wanted. To Sydney Morris and Kell Wilson at Simon & Schuster, we are writing these acknowledgments well before the press tour, but we know we will have *much* to be grateful for by the time we hit pub day. Also on the PR front, thank you so much to the brands who partnered with us for your generosity in helping to support this book. It takes a village, and you've made this village very chic.

As we've said, it takes a village, so we need to thank ours. We are infinitely grateful to our own civic pod, our friends who have influenced this book in countless intangible ways. Thank you for keeping us sane in these unprecedented times.

Sami: I am endlessly grateful every day for my entire team at Betches, present and past: you are the best of the best. Aleen and Jordana, I count myself among the luckiest in the world to be part of our rare combination of business partners, friends, sisters, and three-headed monster. Thank you for believing in my writing and entertaining my fears about dictators. Same to Solly and the lads at LBG Media: thank you so much for your support and encouragement. And to Jonathan, there's no way I can quantify everything you've taught me over the past 13 years, but I'm sure *you* can, since you're the accountant.

To everyone who has been part of the Betches Sup/Betches News journey, you have all influenced this book, and your humor has done more to save democracy than our Supreme Court (not that high a bar but still). And Michelle, where would I be if we hadn't bonded over Magic Sleek and keto years ago?

Avi, you're my cheerleader and my backbone. Thank you for being my partner in every way, whether writing a book or making breakfast (can't be good at everything). I love you and am endlessly grateful for all we've built together.

Mom, you are the reason I could write this book. Thanks to you, I was too young to remember my first time in a voting booth. Thanks to you, I rarely miss a headline for the Morning Announcements. You've helped me see all the invisible ways that politics and civics show up in our lives. Thank you for all the lessons you taught me in raising Zach. You've shown me that there are many ways to change lives. I'm grateful for every day we spend together and for everything that you and our family have sacrificed for me. You've never let me forget what a privilege it is to be an American, even when I was in college and insisted my vote didn't count because we're from New York.

And finally, thank you to my coauthor and my dear friend, both in and out of my phone, Emily. Your vast knowledge and fervent dedication to making practical progress have taught me that it *is* possible to get things done in government, despite how chaotic and dire things appear. Your contribution to our democracy is incalculable, and we're all going to be better-off thanks to your tireless work.

Emily: A big thank-you to the EYP audience who gives *me* the hope that we can build a better tomorrow. You've helped me feel more confident in my voice, and for that I am forever grateful. To all my friends in and out of my phone, I'm so thankful for the counsel, emotional sustenance, laughs, and ideas you have offered in this season and all others.

Massachusetts state rep Alice Peisch gave me my first job in politics (an internship in her office) and encouraged me to run for local office at age 20. (I won!) The Schumer office, who taught me how to get the wheels turning in Congress. And my favorite coworker, Ed MacAllister, who has supported all my civic dreams. A hearty thanks.

Biggest thanks go to my parents. My dad has always been there through three graduate degrees, countless career pivots, a bunch of pets, many moves, and more with tremendous love and a constant reminder that his advice is always best. And my mother, who though she died 20 years ago continues to shape my life every day. I regularly think about two key civic lessons she taught me when I was a young child: (1) She brought me along as she volunteered for the campaign of our local State House candidate—knocking on doors, stuffing envelopes, and helping set up events—teaching me that I had a place in our political process; (2) she helped me pitch PBS on a kids TV show, even though it had no chance of happening—teaching me that she always believed that my voice deserved to be heard in the room.

And a mighty thanks to my coauthor and friend in and outside of our feeds, Sami. You thrive on making big ideas happen, and there's nothing bigger than saving our democracy. So proud to walk with you in this fight.

ENDNOTES

★ ★ ★ ★ ★

WHY WE'RE HERE

1   Hannah Hartig et al., "Republican Gains in 2022 Midterms Driven Mostly by Turnout Advantage," Pew Research Center, July 12, 2023, accessed March 31, 2024, https://www.pewresearch.org/politics/2023/07/12/republican-gains-in-2022-midterms-driven-mostly-by-turnout-advantage/.

WHY HELPING DEMOCRACY WILL ALSO GIVE YOU A MORE MEANINGFUL LIFE

1   Robert D. Putnam, *Bowling Alone: The Collapse and Revival of American Community* (New York: Simon & Schuster, 2000), 332. See also Iain McGilchrist, "The Curvilinearity of Life," *Psychology Today*, December 4, 2010, https://www.psychologytoday.com/us/blog/the-skeptical-brain/201012/the-curvilinearity-life.

2   Robert D. Putnam and Lewis Feldstein, *Better Together: Restoring the American Community.* (New York: Simon & Schuster, 2009), 49.

3   Brad Stulburg, "Extended Loneliness Can Make You More Vulnerable to Extremist Views," *Time*, November 3, 2022, https://time.com/6223229/loneliness-vulnerable-extremist-views.

ON DEMOCRACY: A WORK IN PROGRESS

1   "Life Expectancy in the U.S. Dropped for the Second Year in a Row in 2021," Centers for Disease Control, August 31, 2022, accessed March 31, 2024, https://www.cdc.gov/nchs/pressroom/nchs_press_releases/2022/20220831.htm.

2   "Hillary Clinton Officially Wins Popular Vote by Nearly 2.9 Million," ABC News, December 22, 2016, https://abcnews.go.com/Politics/hillary-clinton-officially-wins-popular-vote-29-million/story?id=44354341.

3   Julia Kirschenbaum and Michael Li, "Gerrymandering Explained," Brennan Center for Justice, June 9, 2023, accessed March 31, 2024, https://www.brennancenter.org/our-work/research-reports/gerrymandering-explained.

4 "Where We Have Been: The History of Gerrymandering in America," in Lee Drutman, "What We Know About Redistricting and Redistricting Reform," New America, September 19, 2022, accessed March 28, 2024, https://www.newamerica.org/political-reform/reports/what-we-know-about-redistricting-and-redistricting-reform/where-we-have-been-the-history-of-gerrymandering-in-america.

5 Ibid.

6 "Guide to Public Financing Programs Nationwide," Brennan Center for Justice, June 29, 2023, https://www.brennancenter.org/our-work/research-reports/guide-public-financing-programs-nationwide.

7 Eric McDaniel, "Congress Wasn't Very Productive in 2023. Here Are the 27 Bills It Passed," NPR, December 29, 2023, https://www.npr.org/2023/12/29/1222245114/congress-wasnt-very-productive-in-2023-here-are-the-27-bills-it-passed.

8 Stephen Hawkins et. al., *Hidden Tribes: A Study of America's Polarized Landscape*, 2018, accessed March 31, 2024, https://hiddentribes.us/media/qfpekz4g/hidden_tribes_report.pdf.

9 Victoria Balara, "Fox News Poll: Voters Favor Gun Limits over Arming Citizens to Reduce Gun Violence," Fox News, April 27, 2023, https://www.foxnews.com/official-polls/fox-news-poll-voters-favor-gun-limits-arming-citizens-reduce-gun-violence.

10 Rani Molla, "Polling Is Clear: Americans Want Gun Control," *Vox*, June 1, 2022, https://www.vox.com/policy-and-politics/23141651/gun-control-american-approval-polling.

11 Vianney Gómez and Bradley Jones, "As Covid-19 Cases Increase, Most Americans Support 'No Excuse' Absentee Voting," Pew Research Center, July 20, 2020, https://www.pewresearch.org/short-reads/2020/07/20/as-covid-19-cases-increase-most-americans-support-no-excuse-absentee-voting.

12 "ABA Survey Finds Support for Election Holiday, Expanded Polling Hours, Voter IDs," American Bar Association, April 29, 2022, https://www.americanbar.org/news/abanews/aba-news-archives/2022/04/aba-survey-finds-support-for-election-holiday.

13 Hannah Hartig, "About Six-in-Ten Americans Say Abortion Should Be Legal in All or Most Cases," Pew Research Center, June 13, 2022, https://www.pewresearch.org/short-reads/2022/06/13/about-six-in-ten-americans-say-abortion-should-be-legal-in-all-or-most-cases-2.

14 "More Acceptance but Growing Polarization on LGBTQ Rights: Findings from the 2022 American Values Atlas," PRRI, March 23, 2023, https://www.prri.org/research/findings-from-the-2022-american-values-atlas.

15 Kim Parker et al, "Americans' Complex Views on Gender Identity and Transgender Issues," Pew Research Center, June 28, 2022, https://www.pewresearch.org/social-trends/2022/06/28/ americans-complex-views-on-gender-identity-and-transgender-issues.

16 Alec Tyson, Cary Funk, and Brian Kennedy, "What the Data Says About Americans' Views of Climate Change," Pew Research Center, August 9, 2023, https://www.pewresearch.org/short-reads/2023/08/09/ what-the-data-says-about-americans-views-of-climate-change.

17 Ali Almelhem et al., *Enlightenment Ideals and Belief in Progress in the Run-up to the Industrial Revolution: A Textual Analysis*, IZA Institute of Labor Economics, December 2023, https://docs.iza.org/dp16674.pdf.

18 Emily Kubin et al, "Personal Experiences Bridge Moral and Political Divides Better Than Facts," *Proceedings of the National Academy of Sciences* 118, no. 6 (January 25, 2021): e2008389118, https://www.pnas.org/doi/full/10.1073/pnas.2008389118.

HOPELESSNESS IS A CIVIC ENGAGEMENT KILLER

1 Charlotte Huff, "Media Overload Is Hurting Our Mental Health. Here Are Ways to Manage Headline Stress," American Psychological Association, November 1, 2022, https://www.apa.org/monitor/2022/11/ strain-media-overload.

2 Reid Hastie and Cass R. Sunstein, "Polarization: One Reason Groups Fail," *Chicago Booth Review*, July 21, 2015, https://www.chicagobooth.edu/ review/one-reason-groups-fail-polarization.

ACTION IS THE ANTIDOTE TO DESPAIR

1 Aaron Schein, "Friend-to-Friend Texting Increases Voter Turnout," Columbia University Data Science Institute, October 28, 2020, https://datascience.columbia.edu/news/2020/friend-to-friend-texting-increases-voter-turnout/.

2 Anaïs Tuepker et al., "The Impacts of Relational Organizing for Health System and Community Collaboration: Early Evidence from a Rapid Multisite Qualitative Study," *Health Services Research* 59, suppl 1 (February 2024): e14256, https://www.ncbi.nlm.nih.gov/pmc/articles/ PMC10796278/.

WHAT IS A CIVIC PERSONALITY?

1 Kelly-Ann Allen et al., "The Need to Belong: A Deep Dive into the Origins, Implications, and Future of a Foundational Construct," *Educational Psychological Review* 34, no. 2 (August 31, 2022): 1133–1156, https://www.ncbi.nlm.nih.gov/pmc/articles/PMC8405711/.

2 Jaruwan Sakulku and James Alexander, "The Impostor Phenomenon," *International Journal of Behavioral Science* 6, no. 1 (2011): 73–92, https://www.sciencetheearth.com/uploads/2/4/6/5/24658156/2011_sakulku_the_impostor_phenomenon.pdf.

CONNECTORS / WATER

1 *Our Epidemic of Loneliness and Isolation 2023: The U.S. Surgeon General's Advisory on the Healing Effects of Social Connection and Community*, Office of the U.S. Surgeon General, accessed March 31, 2024, https://www.hhs.gov/sites/default/files/surgeon-general-social-connection-advisory.pdf.

2 Hannah Arendt, *The Origins of Totalitarianism* (Cleveland: Meridian Books, 1962), 323–324.

CREATORS / AIR

1 Alex Hopper, "Behind the Band Name: The Cranberries," 2023, *American Songwriter*, https://americansongwriter.com/behind-the-band-name-the-cranberries/.

2 Ben Beaumont-Thomas, "Carl Bean, Singer of Gay Pride Anthem I Was Born This Way, Dies Aged 77," *Guardian*, September 8, 2021, https://www.theguardian.com/music/2021/sep/08/carl-bean-singer-i-was-born-this-way-dies-aged-77.

BUILD A CIVIC NETWORK WITHOUT "NETWORKING"

1 SAIC Multicultural Affairs, "Lesson 5: Radical Self Care," in *Learn and Unlearn: Anti-Racism Resource Guide*, School of the Art Institute of Chicago, February 2022, https://libraryguides.saic.edu/learn_unlearn/wellness5.

HOW THE GOVERNMENT WORKS

1 Zack Beauchamp, "Sen. Mike Lee's Tweets Against 'Democracy,' Explained," *Vox*, October 8, 2020, https://www.vox.com/policy-and-politics/21507713/mike-lee-democracy-republic-trump-2020.

2 "Statement of Concern: The Threats to American Democracy and the Need for National Voting and Election Administration Standards," New America, June 1, 2021, https://www.newamerica.org/political-reform/statements/statement-of-concern/.

3 "Historical Apportionment Data (1910–2020)," United States Census Bureau, April 26, 2021, https://www.census.gov/data/tables/time-series/dec/apportionment-data-text.html.